Rick Steves®

SNAPSHOT

W9-BOO-067

Northern Ireland

CONTENTS

Belfast

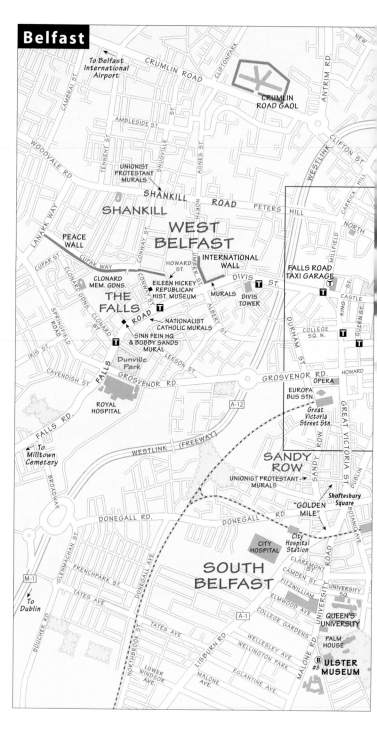

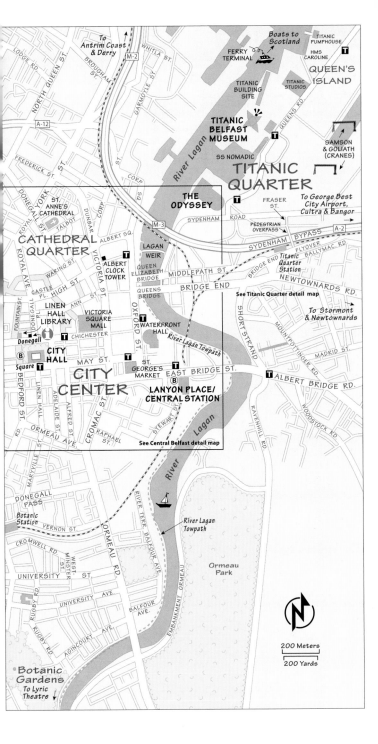

To Antrim Coast & Derry

Boats to Scotland

TITANIC PUMPHOUSE

FERRY TERMINAL

HMS CAROLINE

QUEEN'S ISLAND

WHITLA ST.

BROUGHAM ST.

GARMOYLE ST.

M-2

NORTH QUEEN ST.

LODGE RD.

A-12

FREDERICK ST.

CORP. SQ.

River Lagan

TITANIC BUILDING SITE

TITANIC STUDIOS

Queens Rd.

TITANIC BELFAST MUSEUM

SS NOMADIC

SAMSON & GOLIATH (CRANES)

TITANIC QUARTER

ST. ANNE'S CATHEDRAL

YORK ST.

ROYAL AVE.

TALBOT

DUNBAR

CORP. ST.

THE ODYSSEY

M-3

FRASER ST.

To George Best City Airport, Cultra & Bangor

CATHEDRAL QUARTER

ALBERT SQ.

SYDENHAM

PEDESTRIAN OVERPASS

SYDENHAM BYPASS

A-2

FLYOVER

WARING ST.

VICTORIA ST.

ALBERT CLOCK TOWER

LAGAN WEIR

Queen Elizabeth Bridge

MIDDLEPATH ST.

BRIDGE END

Titanic Quarter Station

BRIDGE END

BALLYMAC. RD.

NEWTOWNARDS RD.

To Stormont & Newtownards

CASTLE PL.

HIGH ST.

ANN ST.

DONEGALL PL.

ROYAL AVE.

FOUNTAIN ST.

Queens Bridge

BRIDGE END

See Titanic Quarter detail map

LINEN HALL LIBRARY

VICTORIA SQUARE MALL

OXFORD ST.

CHICHESTER

Donegall

WATERFRONT HALL

River Lagan Towpath

SHORT STRAND

MOUNTPOTTINGER RD.

MADRID ST.

CITY HALL

MAY ST.

ST. GEORGE'S MARKET

EAST BRIDGE ST.

ALBERT BRIDGE RD.

B Square

CITY CENTER

LANYON PLACE/ CENTRAL STATION

RAVENHILL RD.

WOODSTOCK RD.

BEDFORD ST.

LINEN HALL

ADELAIDE ST.

ALFRED ST.

CROMAC ST.

RAPHAEL ST.

STEWART ST.

ORMEAU AVE.

River Lagan

See Central Belfast detail map

MARYVILLE ST.

DONEGALL PASS

Botanic Station

VERNON ST.

ORMEAU RD.

RIVER TERR.

BALFOUR AVE.

EMBANKMENT ORMEAU

River Lagan Towpath

Ormeau Park

CROMWELL RD.

WEST MINSTER ST.

UNIVERSITY ST.

UNIVERSITY AVE.

BALFOUR AVE.

RUGBY RD.

AGINCOURT AVE.

RUGBY RD.

Botanic Gardens

To Lyric Theatre

200 Meters

200 Yards

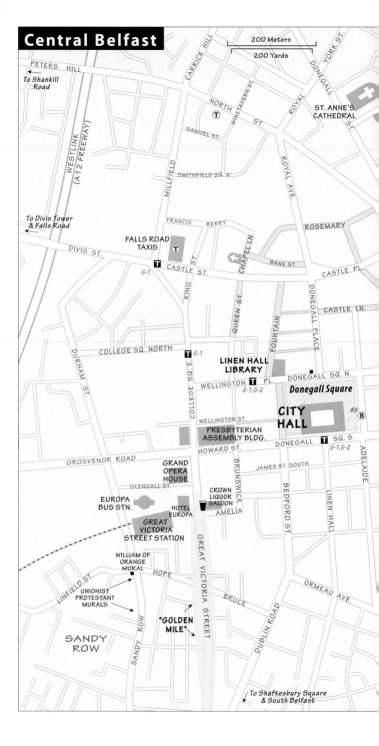

Central Belfast

200 Meters
200 Yards

PETERS HILL

To Shankill Road

WESTLINK (A12 FREEWAY)

CARRICK HILL

YORK ST.

DONEGALL

ST. ANNE'S CATHEDRAL

NORTH ST.

WINETAVERN ST.

ROYAL

SAMUEL ST.

SMITHFIELD SQ. N.

MILLFIELD

ROYAL AVE.

ROSEMARY

To Divis Tower & Falls Road

FRANCIS

BERRY

FALLS ROAD TAXIS

DIVIS ST.

CASTLE ST.

CHAPEL LN.

BANK ST.

G-1

KING ST.

QUEEN ST.

CASTLE PL.

CASTLE LN.

COLLEGE SQ. NORTH

DURHAM ST.

COLLEGE SQ. E.

G-1

FOUNTAIN

DONEGALL PLACE

LINEN HALL LIBRARY

WELLINGTON PL.

G-1, G-2

DONEGALL SQ. N.

Donegall Square

CITY HALL

#B

WELLINGTON ST.

PRESBYTERIAN ASSEMBLY BLDG.

DONEGALL SQ. S.

G-1, G-2

GROSVENOR ROAD

HOWARD ST.

BRUNSWICK

JAMES ST. SOUTH

ADELAIDE

GRAND OPERA HOUSE

GLENGALL ST.

BEDFORD ST.

LINEN HALL

EUROPA BUS STN.

HOTEL EUROPA

CROWN LIQUOR SALOON

AMELIA

GREAT VICTORIA STREET STATION

WILLIAM OF ORANGE MURAL

HOPE

ORMEAU AVE.

LINFIELD ST.

UNIONIST PROTESTANT MURALS

SANDY ROW

SANDY ROW

"GOLDEN MILE"

GREAT VICTORIA STREET

BRUCE

DUBLIN ROAD

To Shaftesbury Square & South Belfast

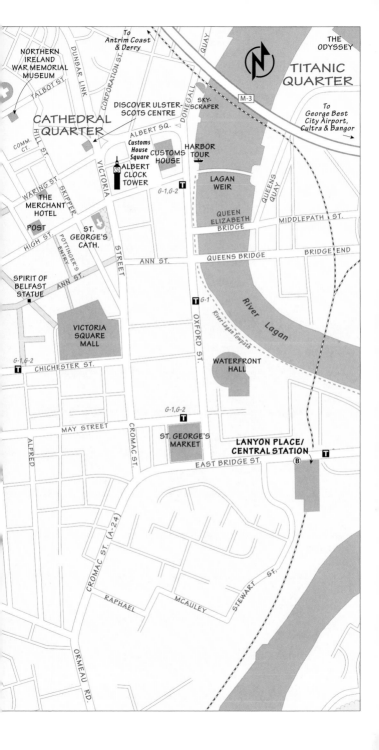

INTRODUCTION

This Snapshot guide, excerpted from my guidebook *Rick Steves Ireland*, introduces you to Northern Ireland—an underrated and often overlooked part of the Emerald Isle that surprises visitors with its friendliness. I've included a lively mix of cities (Belfast and Derry), smaller towns (Portrush and Bangor), and plenty of lazy rural sights. History is palpable atop the brooding walls of Derry and in the remote and traditional countryside. And, while it's perfectly safe for a visit, Northern Ireland gives you a feel for Ireland's 20th-century "Troubles" as nowhere else—especially the provocative political murals in Derry's Bogside neighborhood, and on Belfast's Falls Road and Shankill Road. You'll also find enjoyable escapes: From the breezy seaside resort of Portrush, you can visit the scenic Antrim Coast—which boasts the unique staggered-columns geology of the Giant's Causeway, the spectacularly set Dunluce Castle, and a chance to sample whiskey at Old Bushmills Distillery.

To help you have the best trip possible, I've included the following topics in this book:

• **Planning Your Time,** with advice on how to make the most of your limited time

• **Orientation,** including tourist information (abbreviated as TI), tips on public transportation, local tour options, and helpful hints

• **Sights** with ratings:

▲▲▲—Don't miss

▲▲—Try hard to see

▲—Worthwhile if you can make it

No rating—Worth knowing about

• **Sleeping** and **Eating,** with good-value recommendations in every price range

• **Connections,** with tips on trains, buses, and driving

Practicalities, near the end of this book, has information on money, staying connected, hotel reservations, transportation, and more.

To travel smartly, read this little book in its entirety before you go. It's my hope that this guide will make your trip more meaningful and rewarding. Traveling like a temporary local, you'll get the absolute most out of every mile, minute, and dollar.

Happy travels!

Rick Steves

NORTHERN IRELAND

NORTHERN IRELAND

Northern Ireland is a different country than the Republic—both politically (it's part of the United Kingdom) and culturally (a combination of Irish, Scottish, and English influences). Occupying the northern one-sixth of the island of Ireland, it's only about 13 miles from Scotland at the narrowest point of the North Channel, and bordered on the south and west by the Republic.

At the moment, that border is almost invisible. But when you leave the Republic of Ireland and enter Northern Ireland, you *are* crossing an international border (although you don't have to flash your passport). The 2016 British referendum vote to leave the EU may change the way this border crossing is handled in the future (see "The Brexit Effect" sidebar, later).

You won't use euros here; Northern Ireland issues its own Ulster pound, which, like the Scottish pound, is interchangeable with the English pound (€1=about £0.90; £1=about $1.30). Price differences create a lively daily shopping trade for those living near the border. Some establishments near the border may take euros, but at a lousy exchange rate. Keep any euros for your return to the Republic, and get pounds from an ATM inside Northern Ireland instead. And if you're heading to Britain next, it's best to change your Ulster pounds into English ones (free at any bank in Northern Ireland, England, Wales, or Scotland).

A generation ago, Northern Ireland was a sadly contorted corner of the world. On my first visit, I remember thinking that even the name of this region sounded painful ("Ulster" seemed to me like a combination of "ulcer" and "blister"). But today, Northern Ireland has emerged from the dark shadow of the decades-long political strife and violence known as the Troubles.

Some differences between Northern Ireland and the Republic are disappearing: Following the Republic's lead, Northern Ireland legalized same-sex marriage and decriminalized abortion in 2019 (also bringing its legislation more in line with rest of the United Kingdom).

And while not as popular among tourists as its neighbor to the south, Northern Ireland offers plenty to see and do...and learn.

Northern Ireland Almanac

Official Name: Northern Ireland (pronounced "Norn Iron" by locals). Some call it Ulster (although historically that term included three counties that today lie on the Republic's side of the border), while others label it the Six Counties.

Size: 5,400 square miles (about the size of Connecticut), constituting a sixth of the island. With 1.8 million people, it's the smallest of the four United Kingdom countries (the others are England, Wales, and Scotland).

Geography: Northern Ireland is shaped roughly like a doughnut, with the UK's largest lake in the middle (Lough Neagh, 150 square miles and a prime eel fishery). Gently rolling hills of green grass rise to the 2,800-foot Slieve Donard. The weather is temperate, cloudy, moist, windy, and hard to predict.

Latitude and Longitude: 54°N and 5°W (as far north as parts of the Alaskan panhandle).

Biggest Cities: Belfast, the capital, has 300,000 residents. Half a million people—nearly one in three Northern Irish—inhabit the greater Belfast area. Derry (called Londonderry by Unionists) has 95,000 people.

Economy: Northern Ireland's economy is more closely tied to the UK than to the Republic of Ireland, and is subsidized by the UK. Traditional agriculture (potatoes and grain) is fading fast, though modern techniques and abundant grassland make Northern Ireland a major producer of sheep, cows, and grass seed. Modern software and communications companies are replacing traditional manufacturing. Shipyards are rusty relics, and the linen industry is now threadbare (both victims of cheaper labor elsewhere).

Government: Northern Ireland is not a self-governing nation, but is part of the UK, ruled from London by Queen Elizabeth II

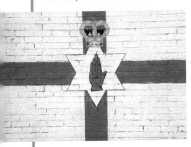

and Prime Minister Boris Johnson, and represented by 18 elected Members of Parliament. For 50 years (1922-1972), Northern Ireland was granted a great deal of autonomy and self-governance, known as "Home Rule." Today some decisions are delegated to a National Assembly (90-seat Parliament), but political logjams often render it ineffective.

Flag: The official flag of Northern Ireland is the Union flag of the UK. But you'll also see the green, white, and orange Irish tricolor (waved by Nationalists) and the Northern Irish flag (white with a red cross and a red hand at its center), which is used by Unionists (see "The Red Hand of Ulster" sidebar on page 92).

The North is affordable, the roads are great, and it's small enough to get a real feel for the place on a short visit. Fishers flock to the labyrinth of lakes in County Fermanagh, hikers seek out County Antrim coastal crags, and those of Scots-Irish descent explore their ancestral farmlands (some of the best agricultural land on the island). Residents (of all stripes) will likely know you're not a local and try hard to be friendly and helpful. It's a region as passionate about its sports and literature as it is about its medieval ruins and Industrial Revolution triumphs.

Having said this, it's important for visitors to Northern Ireland to understand the ways in which its population is segregated along political, religious, and cultural lines. Roughly speaking, the eastern seaboard is more Unionist, Protestant, and of English-Scottish heritage, while the south and west (bordering the Republic of Ireland) are Nationalist, Catholic, and of indigenous Irish descent. Cities are often clearly divided between neighborhoods of one group or the other. Early in life, locals learn to identify the highly symbolic (and highly charged) colors, jewelry, sports jerseys, music, names, accents, and vocabulary that distinguish the cultural groups.

Over the last century, the conflict between these two groups has not been solely about faith. Heated debates today are usually about politics: Will Northern Ireland stay part of the United Kingdom (Unionists), or become part of the Republic of Ireland (Nationalists)?

The roots of Protestant and Catholic differences date back to the time when Ireland was a colony of Great Britain. Four hundred years ago, Protestant settlers from England and Scotland were strategically "planted" in Catholic Ireland to help assimilate the island into the British economy. In 1620, the dominant English powerbase in London felt entitled to call both islands—Ireland as well as Britain—the "British Isles" on maps (a geographic label that irritates Irish Nationalists to this day). These Protestant settlers established their own cultural toehold on the island, laying claim to the most fertile land. Might made right, and God was on their side. Meanwhile, the underdog Catholic Irish held strong to their Gaelic culture on their ever-diminishing, boggy, rocky farms.

By the beginning of the 20th century, the sparse Protestant population could no longer control the entire island. When Ireland won its independence in 1921 (after a bloody guerrilla war against British rule), 26 of the island's 32 counties became the Irish Free State, ruled from Dublin with dominion status in the British Commonwealth—similar to Canada's level of sovereignty. In 1949, these 26 counties left the Commonwealth altogether and became the Republic of Ireland, severing all political ties with Britain. Meanwhile, the six remaining northeastern counties—the only ones with a Protestant majority who considered themselves Brit-

ish—chose not to join the Irish Free State and remained part of the UK.

But within these six counties—now joined as the political entity called Northern Ireland—was a large, disaffected Irish (mostly Catholic) minority who felt marginalized by the drawing of the new international border. This sentiment was represented by the Irish Republican Army (IRA), who wanted all 32 of Ireland's counties to be united in one Irish nation—their political goals were "Nationalist." Their political opponents were the "Unionists"—Protestant British eager to defend the union with Britain, who were primarily led by two groups: the long-established Orange Order, and the military muscle of the newly mobilized Ulster Volunteer Force (UVF).

In World War II, the Republic stayed neutral while the North enthusiastically supported the Allied cause—winning a spot close to London's heart. Derry (a.k.a. Londonderry) became an essential Allied convoy port, while Belfast lost more than 900 civilians during four Luftwaffe bombing raids in 1941. After the war, the split between North and South seemed permanent, and Britain invested heavily in Northern Ireland to bring it solidly into the UK fold.

In the Republic of Ireland (the South), where the population was 94 percent Catholic and only 6 percent Protestant, there was a clearly dominant majority. But in the North, Catholics were a sizable 35 percent of the population—enough to demand attention when they exposed anti-Catholic discrimination on the part of the Protestant government. It was this discrimination that led to the Troubles, the conflict that filled headlines from the late 1960s to the late 1990s.

Partly inspired by Martin Luther King, Jr. and the civil rights movement in America, in the 1960s the Catholic minority in Northern Ireland began a nonviolent struggle to end discrimination, advocating for better jobs and housing. Extremists polarized issues, and once-peaceful demonstrations became violent.

Unionists were afraid that if the island became one nation, the relatively poor Republic of Ireland would drag down the comparatively affluent North, and feared losing political power to a Catholic majority. As the two sides clashed in 1969, the British Army entered the fray. Their role, initially a peacekeeping one, gradually evolved into acting as muscle for the Unionist government. In 1972, a tragic watershed year, more than 500 people died as combatants moved from petrol bombs to guns, and a new, more violent IRA emerged. In the 30-year (1968-1998) chapter of the struggle for an independent and united Ireland, more than 3,000 people died.

In the 1990s—with the UK (and Ireland's) membership in the EU, the growth of its economy, and the weakening of the Catholic Church's authority—the Republic of Ireland's influence became less threatening to the Unionists. Optimists hailed the signing of a breakthrough peace plan in 1998, called the "Good Friday Peace Accord" by Nationalists, or the "Belfast Agreement" by Unionists. This led to the release of political prisoners on both sides in 2000—a highly emotional event.

British Army surveillance towers in Northern Ireland's cities were dismantled in 2006, and the army formally ended its 38-year-long Operation Banner campaign in 2007. In 2010, the peace process was jolted forward by a surprisingly forthright apology offered by then-British Prime Minister David Cameron, who expressed regret for the British Army's offenses on Bloody Sunday (see sidebar on page 24). The apology was prompted by the Saville Report—the results of an investigation conducted by the UK government as part of the Good Friday Peace Accord. It found that the 1972 shootings of Nationalist civil-rights marchers on Bloody Sunday by British soldiers was "unjustified" and the victims innocent (vindication for the victims' families, who had fought since 1972 to clear their loved ones' names).

Major hurdles to a lasting peace persist. Occasionally back-

Northern Ireland Terminology

You may hear Northern Ireland referred to as **Ulster**—the traditional name of Ireland's ancient northernmost province. When the Republic of Ireland became independent in 1922, six of the nine counties of Ulster elected to form Northern Ireland, while three counties joined the Republic.

The mostly Protestant **Unionist** majority—and the more hardline, working-class **Loyalists**—want the North to remain in the UK. The **Ulster Unionist Party** (UUP) is the political party representing moderate Unionist views (Nobel Peace Prize co-winner David Trimble led the UUP from 1995 to 2005). The **Democratic Unionist Party** (DUP) takes a harder stance in defense of Unionism. The **Ulster Volunteer Force** (UVF), the **Ulster Freedom Fighters** (UFF), and the **Ulster Defense Association** (UDA) are Loyalist paramilitary organizations: All three are labeled "proscribed groups" by the UK's 2000 Terrorism Act.

The mostly Catholic **Nationalist** minority—and the more hardline, working-class **Republicans**—want a united and independent Ireland ruled by Dublin. The **Social Democratic Labor Party** (SDLP), founded by Nobel Peace Prize co-winner John Hume, is the moderate political party representing Nationalist views. **Sinn Féin** takes a harder stance in defense of Nationalism. The **Irish Republican Army** (IRA) is the now-disarmed Nationalist paramilitary organization historically linked with Sinn Féin. The **Alliance Party** wants to bridge the gap between Unionists and Nationalists.

The long-simmering struggle to settle Northern Ireland's national identity precipitated the **Troubles,** the violent, 30-year conflict (1968-1998) between Unionist and Nationalist factions. To gain more insight into the complexity of the Troubles, the 90-minute documentary *Voices from the Grave* provides an excellent overview (easy to find on YouTube). Also check out the University of Ulster's informative and evenhanded Conflict Archive at https://cain.ulster.ac.uk.

Northern Ireland Politics

NATIONALISTS
(MOSTLY CATHOLICS)
"Feel Irish"

UNIONISTS
(MOSTLY PROTESTANTS)
"Feel British"

SINN FEIN   ALLIANCE   DUP

SDLP   UUP
John Hume   David Trimble
(retired)   (retired)

MODERATES

REPUBLICANS   LOYALISTS

GREEN   ORANGE

Not to scale &
not all opinions shown

ward-thinking extremists ape the brutality of their grandparents' generation. But the downtown checkpoints and "bomb-damage clearance sales" are long gone, replaced by a forest of construction cranes, especially in rejuvenated Belfast. Tourists in Northern Ireland were once considered courageous (or reckless). Today, more tourists than ever are venturing north to Belfast and Derry, and cruise-ship crowds disembark in Belfast to board charter buses that fan out to visit the Giant's Causeway and Old Bushmills Distillery.

When locals spot you with a map and a lost look on your face, they're likely to ask, "Wot yer lookin fer?" in their distinctive Northern accent. They're not suspicious of you, but trying to help you find your way. They may even "giggle" (Google) it for you. You're safer in Belfast than in many UK cities—and far safer, statistically, than in most major US cities. You'd have to look for trouble to find it here. Just don't seek out spit-and-sawdust pubs in working-class neighborhoods and spew simplistic opinions about sensitive local topics. Tourists notice lingering tension mainly during the "marching season" (Easter-Aug, peaking in early July). July 12—"the Twelfth"—is traditionally the most confrontational day of the year in the North, when proud Protestant Unionist Orangemen march to celebrate their Britishness (often through staunchly Nationalist Catholic neighborhoods—it's still good advice to lie low if you stumble onto any big Orange parades).

As the less-fractured Northern Ireland enters the 21st century, one of its most valuable assets is its industrious people (the "Protestant work ethic"). When they emigrated to the US, they became known as the Scots-Irish and played a crucial role in our nation's founding. They were signers of our Declaration of Independence, a dozen of our presidents (think tough-as-nails "Old Hickory" Andrew Jackson as a classic example), and the ancestors of Davy Crockett and Mark Twain.

Northern Irish workers have a proclivity for making things that go. They've produced far-reaching inventions like Dunlop's first inflatable tire. The Shorts aircraft factory (in Belfast) built the Wright Brothers' first aircraft for commercial sale and the world's first vertical takeoff jet. The *Titanic* was the only flop of Northern Ireland's otherwise successful shipbuilding industry. The once-futuristic DeLorean sports car was made in Belfast.

Notable people from Northern Ireland include musicians Van Morrison and James Galway, and actors Liam Neeson, Roma Downey, Ciarán Hinds, and Kenneth Branagh. The North also produced Christian intellectual and writer C. S. Lewis, Victorian physicist Lord Kelvin, engineer Harry Ferguson (inventor of the modern farm tractor and first four-wheel-drive Formula One car), and soccer-star playboy George Best—who once famously re-

The Brexit Effect

A hundred years ago, the British Isles were ruled from one place: London. Today, parts of this geographic area (Ireland, Scotland, and England/Wales) drift in separate directions. And Northern Ireland, with strong cultural, geographic, and economic connections to all three, is being stretched uncomfortably.

In 2016, the people of the United Kingdom narrowly approved a referendum to leave the European Union ("Brexit"). But in Northern Ireland (as in Scotland), a majority of people voted to remain.

To the west, Scotland is flirting with independence: Separating from the UK would allow it to stay in the EU. (And many among the North's Unionist community trace their ancestry to Scotland.) To the south, the Republic of Ireland (an EU member) fills 80 percent of the island of Ireland; a growing minority in the North would like to see the island come together as a single Irish nation—inside the EU.

Which direction will the North lean? Special status within the UK? Reunification with the Republic?

The Good Friday agreement that ended the Troubles assumed there'd be open borders between Northern Ireland and the Republic. As the UK leaves the EU, one of the largest questions is what form the new border will take. Few want a "hard border," with trade tariffs and border controls between EU and UK zones. For example, the Northern Ireland border city of Derry has a struggling economy that relies on easy access to rural County Donegal, next door in the Republic. Making that market harder to reach would cause further hardship to a vulnerable community.

Beyond the economics, a hard border could add fuel to "them and us" perceptions, rekindling tension between dormant Republican and Loyalist extremists. No one wants to go back to the days when the border between Northern Ireland and the Republic was a closely patrolled line in a war zone.

Some Northern Irelanders are hedging their bets: Anyone born in Northern Ireland is eligible for a British passport, an Irish one, or both. Traditionally, Nationalist Catholics chose an Irish one and Unionist Protestants went for a British one. But with Brexit looming, many staunchly loyal Unionists are quietly opting to get an Irish passport as well to keep their options open.

Stay tuned to see how the swirling currents of Brexit, the Scottish independence movement, and the Irish reunification dream will affect this unique corner of the world...perched precariously between diverging cultural and economic powers: Ireland, Scotland, and England.

marked, "I spent most of my money on liquor and women...and the rest I wasted."

As in the Republic, sports are big in the North. Northern-born golfers Rory McIlroy, Graeme McDowell, and Darren Clarke have won a fistful of majors, filling local hearts with pride. With close ties to Scotland, many Northern Irish fans follow the exploits of Glasgow soccer teams—but which team you root for betrays which side of the tracks you come from. Those who cheer for Glasgow Celtic (green and white) are Nationalist and Catholic; those waving banners for the Glasgow Rangers (blue with red trim) are Unionist and Protestant. To maintain peace, some pubs post signs on their doors banning patrons from wearing sports jerseys. Luckily, sports with no sectarian history are now being introduced, such as the Belfast Giants ice hockey team—a hit with both communities.

Northern Ireland seems poised to do great things. As you travel through Northern Ireland today, you'll encounter a fascinating country with a complicated, often tragic history—and a brightening future.

DERRY

No city in Ireland connects the kaleidoscope of historical dots more colorfully than Derry. From a leafy monastic hamlet to a Viking-pillaged port, from a cannonball-battered siege survivor to an Industrial Revolution sweatshop, from an essential WWII naval base to a wrenching flashpoint of sectarian Troubles... Derry has seen it all.

Though Belfast is the capital of Northern Ireland, this pivotal city has a more diverse history and a prettier setting. Derry was a vibrant city back when Belfast was just a mudflat. With roughly a third of Belfast's population (95,000), Derry feels more welcoming and manageable to visitors.

The town is the mecca of Ulster Unionism. When Ireland was being divvied up, the River Foyle was the logical border between the North and the Republic. But, for sentimental and economic reasons, the North kept Derry, which is otherwise on the Republic's side of the river. Consequently, this predominantly Catholic-Nationalist city was much contested throughout the Troubles.

While most of its population and its city council call it "Derry," some maps, road signs, and all UK train schedules use "Londonderry," the name on its 1662 royal charter and the one favored by Unionists. I once asked a Northern Ireland rail employee for a ticket to "Derry"; he replied that there was no such place, but he would sell me one to "Londonderry." I'll call it Derry in this book since that's what the majority of the city's inhabitants do.

The past 15 years have brought some refreshing changes. Manned British Army surveillance towers were taken down in 2006, and most British troops finally departed in mid-2007, after 38 years in Northern Ireland. In 2011, a curvy pedestrian bridge across the River Foyle was completed. Locals dubbed it the Peace Bridge because it links the predominantly Protestant Waterside (east bank) with the predominantly Catholic Cityside (west bank). Today, you can feel comfortable wandering the streets and enjoying this underrated city.

PLANNING YOUR TIME

If just passing through (say, on your way to Portrush—see the next chapter), it takes a few hours to see the essential Derry sights: Visit the Tower Museum and catch some views from the town wall.

With more time, spend a night in Derry, so you can see the powerful Bogside murals and take a walking tour around the town walls. With two nights in Derry, consider crossing back into the Republic for a scenic driving loop through part of remote County Donegal.

Orientation to Derry

The River Foyle flows north, slicing Derry into eastern and western chunks. The old town walls and almost all worthwhile sights are on the west side. (The tiny train station and Ebrington Square—at the end of the Peace Bridge—are the main reasons to spend time on the east side.) Waterloo Place and the adjacent Guildhall Square, just outside the north corner of the old city walls, are the pedestrian hubs of city activity. The Strand Road area extending north from Waterloo Place makes a comfortable home base, with lodging and restaurant suggestions within a block or two. The Diamond (main square) and its War Memorial statue mark the heart of the old city within the walls.

TOURIST INFORMATION

The TI sits on the riverfront and rents bikes (£5/2 hours, £8/4 hours, £12/8 hours), and can book bus and walking tours (Mon-Fri 9:00-17:30, Sat-Sun 10:00-17:00, closes earlier in off-season; 44 Foyle Street, tel. 028/7126-7284, www.visitderry.com).

ARRIVAL IN DERRY

By Train: Next to the river on the east side of town, Derry's little end-of-the-line train station (no storage lockers) has service to Portrush, Belfast, and Dublin. Each arriving train is greeted by free shuttle buses to Ulsterbus Station on the west side of town, a couple of minutes' walk south of Guildhall Square on Foyle Street (luggage storage at post office around corner in same building, Mon-Fri 9:30-17:30—beware of lunch closure, closed Sat-Sun). Otherwise, it's a £5 taxi ride to Guildhall Square. The same free shuttle service leaves Ulsterbus Station 15 minutes before each departing train.

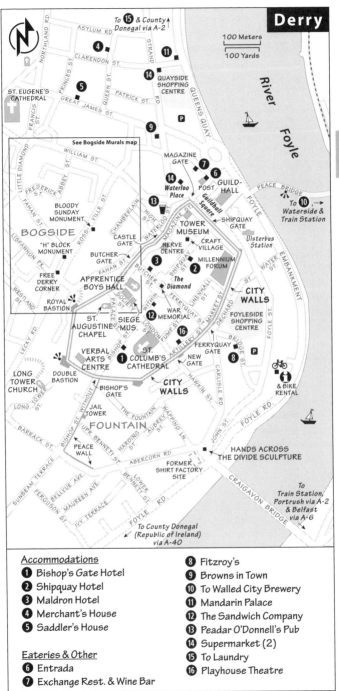

DERRY

Derry

To 15 & County Donegal via A-2

100 Meters
100 Yards

River Foyle

St. Eugene's Cathedral

See Bogside Murals map

BOGSIDE
Bloody Sunday Monument
"H" Block Monument
Free Derry Corner
Royal Bastion
Apprentice Boys Hall

Magazine Gate
Waterloo Place
Post
Guildhall
Guildhall Square
Tower Museum
Nerve Centre
Craft Village
Millennium Forum
The Diamond
War Memorial
Shipquay Gate
Ulsterbus Station
Peace Bridge
To 10 Waterside & Train Station
City Walls

Quayside Shopping Centre

Foyleside Shopping Centre

St. Augustine's Chapel
Siege Mus.
Verbal Arts Centre
St. Columb's Cathedral
Double Bastion
Long Tower Church
Jail Tower
Bishop's Gate
Ferryquay Gate
New Gate
City Walls
& Bike Rental

FOUNTAIN
Peace Wall
Former Shirt Factory Site
Hands Across the Divide Sculpture

To County Donegal (Republic of Ireland) via A-40

To Train Station, Portrush via A-2 & Belfast via A-6

Accommodations
1 Bishop's Gate Hotel
2 Shipquay Hotel
3 Maldron Hotel
4 Merchant's House
5 Saddler's House

Eateries & Other
6 Entrada
7 Exchange Rest. & Wine Bar

8 Fitzroy's
9 Browns in Town
10 To Walled City Brewery
11 Mandarin Palace
12 The Sandwich Company
13 Peadar O'Donnell's Pub
14 Supermarket (2)
15 To Laundry
16 Playhouse Theatre

By Bus: All intercity buses stop at the Ulsterbus Station, on Foyle Street close to Guildhall Square.

By Car: Foyleside parking garage across from the TI is handy for day-trippers (£1/hour, £3/4 hours, Mon-Tue 8:00-19:00, Wed-Fri until 22:00, Sat until 20:00, Sun 12:00-17:00, tel. 028/7137-7323). If staying overnight, ask about parking at your B&B, or try the Quayside parking garage behind the Travelodge (£1/hour, £3/4 hours, £8 additional for overnight, daily 7:30-21:00, closes earlier on weekends).

HELPFUL HINTS

Money: Danske Bank is on Guildhall Square and the Bank of Ireland is on Strand Road.

Bookstore: Foyle Books is a dusty little pleasure for browsing (Mon-Fri 11:00-17:00, Sat 10:00-17:00, closed Sun, 12 Magazine Street at entrance to Craft Village, tel. 028/7137-2530).

Laundry: Bubbles has drop-off service—bring it in the morning, pick up later that day (Mon-Fri 9:00-17:00, Sat from 10:00, closed Sun, 141 Strand Road, tel. 028/7136-3366).

Taxi: Try **City Cabs** (tel. 028/7126-4466), **The Taxi Company** (tel. 028/7126-2626), or **Foyle Taxis** (tel. 028/7127-9999).

Car Rental: Enterprise is handy (70 Clooney Road, tel. 028/7186-1699, www.enterprise.co.uk). Another option is **Desmond Motors** (173 Strand Road, tel. 028/7136-7136, www.desmondmotors.co.uk).

Tours in Derry

Walking Tours

McCrossan's City Tours leads insightful hour-long walks, giving a rounded view of the city's history. Tours depart from 11 Carlisle Road, just below Ferryquay Gate (£4; daily at 10:00, 12:00, 14:00, and 16:00; tel. 028/7127-1996, mobile 077-1293-7997, www.derrycitytours.com, derrycitytours@aol.com). They also offer private group tours (£60).

Bogside History Tours offers walks led by Bogside residents who lost loved ones in the tragic events of Bloody Sunday (£6, £9 combo-ticket with Museum of Free Derry; April-Sept daily at 11:00 and 13:00, in summer also Mon-Fri also at 15:00; departs from in front of the Guildhall, mobile 077-3145-0088 or 078-0056-7165, www.bogsidehistorytours.com, paul@bogsidehistorytours.com). Tour guides also offer various taxi tours (£25/hour, call or email for options).

Bus Tours

Game of Thrones Tours brings you to the beautiful North Antrim Coast, focusing on locations used in the *Game of Thrones* TV series (see sidebar on page 50). Stops included on the all-day tour are Dunluce Castle (photo stop), Carrick-a-Rede Rope Bridge, Giant's Causeway, and the Dark Hedges (photo stop), with a lunch stop in Ballintoy (£40, bus departs Derry TI daily at 8:00, returns by 17:30, no kids under 12, some walking, tel. 028/9568-0023, www. gameofthronestours.com).

City Sightseeing's hop-on, hop-off double-decker buses are a good option for a general overview of Derry. The one-hour loop covers both sides of the river (seven stops overall), including the Guildhall, the old city walls, political wall murals, cathedrals, and former shirt factories. Your ticket is good for 24 hours (£12.50, pay driver, bus departs April-Sept daily on the hour 10:00-16:00 from in front of TI and Guildhall Square, tel. 028/7137-0067, www. citysightseeingderry.com).

City Sightseeing also offers trips from Derry to the Giant's Causeway, Old Bushmills Distillery, and Carrick-a-Rede Rope Bridge in County Antrim (£40, does not include entry fees, runs daily May-Sept, depart TI at 10:00, return by 16:00, minimum 10 people).

Walks in Derry

Though calm today, Derry is stamped by years of tumultuous conflict. These two self-guided walks (less than an hour each) explore the town's history. "Walk the Walls," starting on the old city walls and ending at the Anglican Cathedral, focuses on Derry's early days. My "Bogside Murals Walk" guides you to the city's compelling murals, which document the time of the Troubles. These walks, each worth ▲▲, can be done separately or linked, depending on your time.

WALK THE WALLS

Squatting determinedly in the city center, the old city walls of Derry (built 1613-1618 and still intact, except for wider gates to handle modern vehicles) hold an almost mythic place in Irish history.

It was here in 1688 that a group of brave apprentice boys, some of whom had been shipped to Derry as orphans after the great fire of London in 1666, made their stand. They slammed the city gates shut in the face of the approaching Catholic forces of deposed King

James II. With this act, the boys galvanized the city's indecisive Protestant defenders inside the walls.

Months of negotiations and a grinding 105-day siege followed, during which a third of the 20,000 refugees and defenders crammed into the city perished. The siege was finally broken in 1689, when supply ships broke through a boom stretched across the River Foyle. The sacrifice and defiant survival of the city turned the tide in favor of newly crowned Protestant King William of Orange, who arrived in Ireland soon after and defeated James at the pivotal Battle of the Boyne.

To fully appreciate the walls, take a walk on top of them (free, open from dawn to dusk). Almost 20 feet high and at least as thick, the walls form a mile-long oval loop. The most interesting section is the half-circuit facing the Bogside, starting at Magazine Gate (stairs face the Tower Museum Derry inside the walls) and finishing at Bishop's Gate.

• *Enter the walls at Magazine Gate and find the stairs opposite the Tower Museum. Once atop the walls, head left.*

Walk the wall as it heads uphill, snaking along the earth's contours. In the row of buildings on the left (just before crossing over Castle Gate), you'll see an arch entry into the **Craft Village,** an alley lined with a cluster of cute shops and cafés that showcase the economic rejuvenation of Derry (Mon-Sat 9:30-17:30, closed Sun).

• *After crossing over Butcher Gate, stop in front of the grand building with the four columns to view the...*

First Derry Presbyterian Church: This impressive-looking building is the second church to occupy this site. The first was built by Queen Mary in the 1690s to thank the Presbyterian community for standing by their Anglican brethren during the dark days of the famous siege. That church was later torn down to make room for today's stately Neoclassical, red-sandstone church finished in 1780. Over the next 200 years, time took its toll on the structure, which was eventually closed due to dry rot and Republican firebombings. But in 2011, the renovated church reopened to a chorus of cross-community approval (yet one more sign of the slow reconciliation taking place in Derry). The **Blue Coat School** exhibit behind the church highlights the important role of Presbyterians in local history (free but donation encouraged, Wed-Fri 11:00-16:00, closed Sat-Tue in summer and all of Oct-April, tel. 028/7126-1550).

• *Just up the block is the...*

Apprentice Boys Memorial Hall: Built in 1873, this houses the private lodge and meeting rooms of an all-male Protestant organization. The group is dedicated to the memory of the original 13 apprentice boys who saved the day during the 1688 siege. Each year, on the Saturday closest to the August 12 anniversary date, the modern-day Apprentice Boys Society celebrates the end of the siege with a controversial march atop the walls. These walls are considered sacred ground for devout Unionists, who claim that many who died during the famous siege were buried within the battered walls because of lack of space. The **Siege Museum** stands behind the hall, giving a narrow-focus Unionist view of the siege (£4, Mon-Sat 10:00-16:30, closed Sun, 18 Society Street, tel. 028/7126-1219).

DERRY

Next, you'll pass a large, square pedestal on the right atop Royal Bastion. It once supported a column in honor of Governor George Walker, the commander of the defenders during the siege. In 1972, the IRA blew up the column, which had 105 steps to the top (one for each day of the siege). An adjacent plaque shows a photo of the column before it was destroyed.

• *Opposite the empty pedestal is the small Anglican...*

St. Augustine Chapel: Set in a pretty graveyard, this Anglican chapel is where some believe the original sixth-century monastery of St. Columba stood. The quaint grounds are open to visitors (Mon-Sat 10:30-16:30, closed Sun except for worship). In Victorian times, this stretch of the walls was a fashionable promenade walk.

As you walk, you'll pass a long wall (on the left)—all that's left of a former **British Army base,** which stood here until 2006. Two 50-foot towers used to loom out of it, bristling with cameras and listening devices. Soldiers built them here for a bird's-eye view of the once-turbulent Catholic Bogside district below. The towers' dismantlement—as well as the removal of most of the British Army from Northern Ireland—is another positive sign in cautiously optimistic Derry. The walls of this former army base now contain a parking lot.

Stop at the **Double Bastion** fortified platform that occupies this corner of the city walls. The old cannon is nicknamed "Roaring Meg" for the fury of its firing during the siege.

From here, you can see across the Bogside to the not-so-far-away hills of County Donegal in the Republic. Derry was once an island, but as the River Foyle gradually changed its course, the area you see below the wall began to drain. Over time, and especially after the Great Potato Famine, Catholic peasants from rural Donegal began to move into Derry to find work during the Industrial Revolution. They settled on this least desirable land...on the soggy bog side of the city. From this vantage point, survey the Bogside with its political murals and Palestinian flags.

DERRY

Derry's History

Once an island in the River Foyle, Derry (from *doire,* Irish for "oak grove") was chosen by St. Columba (St. Colmcille) around AD 546 for a monastic settlement. He later banished himself to the island of Iona in Scotland out of remorse for sparking a bloody battle over the rights to a holy manuscript that he had secretly copied.

A thousand years later, the English defeated the last Ulster-based Gaelic chieftains in the Battle of Kinsale (1601). With victory at hand, the English took advantage of the power vacuum. They began the "plantation" of Ulster with loyal Protestant subjects imported from Scotland and England. The native Irish were displaced to less desirable rocky or boggy lands, sowing the seeds of resentment that eventually fueled the Troubles.

A dozen wealthy London guilds (grocers, haberdashers, tailors, and others) took on Derry as an investment and changed its name to "Londonderry." They built the last great walled city in Ireland to protect their investment from the surrounding—and hostile—Irish locals. The walls proved their worth in 1688-1689, when the town's Protestant defenders, loyal to King William of Orange, withstood a prolonged siege by the forces of Catholic King James II. "No surrender" is still a passionate rallying cry among Ulster Unionists determined to remain part of the United Kingdom.

The town became a major port of emigration to the New World in the early 1800s. Then, when the Industrial Revolution provided a steam-powered sewing factory, the city developed a thriving shirtmaking industry. The factories here employed mostly Catholic women who flocked in from rural County Donegal. Although Belfast grew larger and wealthier, Unionists tightened their grip on "Londonderry" and the walls that they regarded with almost holy reverence. In 1921, they insisted that the city be included in Northern Ireland when the province was partitioned from the new Irish Free State (later to become the Republic of Ireland). A bit of gerrymandering (with three lightly populated Unionist districts outvoting two densely populated Nationalist

Directly below and to the right are Free Derry Corner and Rossville Street, where the tragic events of Bloody Sunday took place. Down on the left is the 18th-century Long Tower Catholic church, named after the monk-built round tower that once stood in the area (see page 32).

• *Head to the grand brick building behind you. This is the...*

districts) ensured that the Protestant minority maintained control of the city, despite its Catholic majority.

Derry was a key escort base for US convoys headed for Britain during World War II, and 60 surviving German U-boats were instructed to surrender here at the end of the war. After the war, poor Catholics—unable to find housing—took over the abandoned military barracks, with multiple families living in each dwelling. Only homeowners were allowed to vote, and the Unionist minority, which controlled city government, was not eager to build more housing that would tip the voting balance away from them. Over the years, sectarian pressures gradually built—until they reached the boiling point. The ugly events of Bloody Sunday on January 30, 1972, brought worldwide attention to the Troubles (see the "Bloody Sunday" sidebar on page 24).

Today, life has stabilized in Derry, and the population has increased by 25 percent in the last 30 years. The 1998 Good Friday Peace Accord made significant progress toward peace, and the British Army withdrew 90 percent of its troops in mid-2007. With a population that is over 70 percent Catholic, the city has agreed to alternate Nationalist and Unionist mayors. There is a feeling of cautious optimism as Derry—the epicenter of bombs and bloody conflicts in the 1960s and 1970s—now boasts a history museum that airs all viewpoints.

The city continues to work on building a happier image. The wall—with all its troubled imagery and once nicknamed "the noose"—is now called "the necklace." With its complicated history, you're damned-if-you-do and damned-if-you-don't when it comes to calling it Derry (pro-Catholic, Nationalist) or Londonderry (pro-Protestant, Unionist). Some call it Derry/Londonderry or Londonderry/Derry. Others just say "Slashtown." And the tourist board calls it "legend-Derry."

Verbal Arts Centre: A former Presbyterian school, this center promotes the development of local literary arts in the form of poetry, drama, writing, and storytelling. Drop in to check the events schedule (Mon-Fri 9:00-17:00, Sat 12:00-14:00, closed Sun, tel. 028/7126-6946, www.verbalartscentre.co.uk).

• *Go another 50 yards around the corner to reach...*

Bishop's Gate: From here, look up Bishop Street Within (inside the walls). This was the site of another British Army surveillance tower. Placed just inside the town walls, it overlooked the neighborhood until 2006. Now look in the other direction to see Bishop Street Without (outside the walls). You'll spot a modern wall topped by a high mesh fence, running along the left side of Bishop Street Without.

This is a so-called **"peace wall,"** built to ensure the security of the Protestant enclave living behind it in Derry's Fountain neighborhood. When the Troubles reignited over 50 years ago, 20,000 Protestants lived on this side of the river. This small housing development of 1,000 people is all that remains of that proud community today. The rest have chosen to move across the river to the mostly Protestant Waterside district. The stone tower halfway down the peace wall is all that remains of the old jail that briefly held doomed rebels after a 1798 revolt against the British.

• *From Bishop's Gate, those short on time can descend from the walls and walk 15 minutes directly back through the heart of the old city, along Bishop Street Within and Shipquay Street to Guildhall Square. With more time, consider visiting St. Columb's Cathedral, the Long Tower Church, and the murals of the Bogside.*

BOGSIDE MURALS WALK

The Catholic Bogside area was the tinderbox of the modern Troubles in Northern Ireland. Bloody Sunday, a terrible confrontation during a march that occurred nearly 50 years ago, sparked a sectarian inferno, and the ashes have not yet fully cooled. Today, the murals of the Bogside give visitors an accessible glimpse of this community's passionate perception of those events.

Getting There: The events are memorialized in 12 murals painted on the ends of residential flats along a 200-yard stretch of Rossville Street and Lecky Road, where the march took place. For the purposes of this walk, you can reach them from Waterloo Place via William Street. They are also accessible from the old city walls at Butcher Gate via the long set of stairs extending below Fahan Street on the grassy hillside, or by the stairs leading down from the Long Tower Church. These days, this neighborhood is gritty but quiet and safe.

The Artists: Two brothers, Tom and William Kelly, and their childhood friend Kevin Hasson are known as the Bogside Artists. They grew up in the Bogside and witnessed the tragic events that

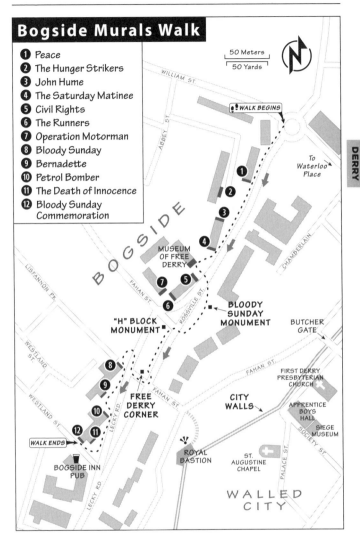

Bogside Murals Walk

1. Peace
2. The Hunger Strikers
3. John Hume
4. The Saturday Matinee
5. Civil Rights
6. The Runners
7. Operation Motorman
8. Bloody Sunday
9. Bernadette
10. Petrol Bomber
11. The Death of Innocence
12. Bloody Sunday Commemoration

50 Meters
50 Yards

WILLIAM ST.

WALK BEGINS

ABBEY ST.

To Waterloo Place

DERRY

BOGSIDE

LISFANNON PK.

FAHAN ST.

MUSEUM OF FREE DERRY

ROSSVILLE ST.

CHAMBERLAIN

BLOODY SUNDAY MONUMENT

"H" BLOCK MONUMENT

BUTCHER GATE

WESTLAND ST.

LECKY RD.

FREE DERRY CORNER

FAHAN ST.

CITY WALLS

FAHAN ST.

FIRST DERRY PRESBYTERIAN CHURCH

APPRENTICE BOYS HALL

SIEGE MUSEUM

SOCIETY ST.

WESTLAND ST.

WALK ENDS

LECKY RD.

ROYAL BASTION

ST. AUGUSTINE CHAPEL

PALACE ST.

BOGSIDE INN PUB

WALLED CITY

took place there, which led them to begin painting the murals in 1994. One of the brothers, Tom, gained a reputation as a "heritage mural" painter, specializing in scenes of life in the old days. In a surprising and hopeful development, Tom was later invited into Derry's Protestant Fountain neighborhood to work with a youth club there on three proud heritage murals that were painted over paramilitary graffiti.

The Murals: Start out at the roundabout intersection of Rossville and William streets.

The Bogside murals face different directions (and some are

Bloody Sunday

Inspired by civil rights marches in America in the mid-1960s, and the Prague Spring uprising and Paris student strikes of 1968, civil rights groups began to protest in Northern Ireland around this time. Initially, their goals were to gain better housing, secure fair voting rights, and end employment discrimination for Catholics in the North. Tensions mounted, and clashes with the predominantly Protestant Royal Ulster Constabulary police force became frequent. Eventually, the British Army was called in to keep the peace.

On January 30, 1972, about 10,000 people protesting internment without trial held an illegal march sponsored by the Northern Ireland Civil Rights Association. British Army barricades kept them from the center of Derry, so they marched through the Bogside neighborhood.

That afternoon, some youths rioted on the fringe of the march. An elite parachute regiment had orders to move in and make arrests in the Rossville Street area. Shooting broke out, and after 25 minutes, 13 marchers were dead and 13 were wounded (one of the wounded later died). The soldiers claimed they came under attack from gunfire and nail-bombs. The marchers said the army shot indiscriminately at unarmed civilians.

The clash, called "Bloody Sunday," uncorked pent-up frustration as moderate Nationalists morphed into staunch Republicans overnight and released a flood of fresh IRA volunteers. An investigation at the time exonerated the soldiers, but the relatives of the victims called it a whitewash and insisted on their innocence.

In 1998, then-British Prime Minister Tony Blair promised a new inquiry, which became the longest and most expensive in British legal history. In 2010, a 12-year investigation—the Saville Report—determined that the Bloody Sunday civil rights protesters were innocent and called the deaths of 14 protesters unjustified.

In a dramatic 2010 speech in the House of Commons, then-British Prime Minister David Cameron apologized to the people of Derry. "What happened on Bloody Sunday was both unjustified and unjustifiable. It was wrong," he declared. Cheers rang out in Derry's Guildhall Square, where thousands had gathered to watch the televised speech. After 38 years, Northern Ireland's bloodiest wound started healing.

partially hidden by buildings), so they're not all visible from a single viewpoint. Plan on walking three long blocks along Rossville Street (which becomes Lecky Road) to see them all. Residents are used to visitors and don't mind if you photograph the murals. Local motorists are uncommonly courteous with allowing visitors to cross the busy street.

From William Street, walk south along the right side of Rossville Street toward Free Derry Corner. The murals will all be on your right.

The first mural you'll walk past is the colorful ❶ *Peace,* showing the silhouette of a dove in flight (left side of mural) and an oak leaf (right side of mural), both created from a single ribbon. A peace campaign asked Derry city schoolchildren to write suggestions for positive peacetime images; their words inspired this artwork. The dove is a traditional symbol of peace, and the oak leaf is a traditional symbol of Derry—recognized by both communities. The dove flies from the sad blue of the past toward the warm yellow of the future.

DERRY

❷ *The Hunger Strikers,* repainted during the summer of 2015, features two Derry-born participants of the 1981 Maze Prison hunger strike, as well as their mothers, who sacrificed and supported them in their fatal decision (10 strikers died). The prison was closed after the release of all prisoners (both Unionist and Nationalist) in 2000.

Smaller and easy to miss (above a ramp with banisters) is ❸ *John Hume.* It's actually a collection of four faces (clockwise from upper left): Nationalist leader John Hume, Martin Luther King, Jr., Nelson Mandela, and Mother Teresa. The Brooklyn Bridge in the middle symbolizes the long-term bridges of understanding that the work of these four Nobel Peace Prize-winning activists created. Born in the Bogside, Hume still maintains a home here.

Now look for ❹ *The Saturday Matinee,* which depicts an outgunned but undaunted local youth behind a screen shield. He holds a stone, ready to throw, while a British armored vehicle approaches (echoing the famous Tiananmen Square photo of the lone Chinese man facing the tank). Why *Saturday Matinee?* It's because the weekend was the best time for locals to engage in a little "recreational rioting" and "have a go at" the army; people were off work and youths were out of school. The "MOFD" at the bottom of this mural stands for the nearby Museum of Free Derry.

Nearby is ❺ *Civil Rights,* showing a marching Derry crowd carrying an anti-sectarian banner. It dates from the days when

Martin Luther King, Jr.'s successful nonviolent marches were being seen worldwide on TV, creating a dramatic, global ripple effect. Civil rights marches, inspired by King and using the same methods to combat a similar set of grievances, gave this long-suffering community a powerful new voice.

All along this walk you'll notice lots of flags, including the red, black, white, and green Palestinian flag. Palestinians and Catholic residents of Northern Ireland have a special empathy for each other—both are indigenous people dealing with the persistent realities of sharing what they consider their rightful homeland with more powerful settlers planted there for political reasons.

In the building behind this mural, you'll find the intense **Museum of Free Derry** (£6, £9 combo-ticket with Bogside History Tours, open Mon-Fri 9:30-16:00 year-round, also open April-Sept Sat-Sun 13:00-16:00, 55 Glenfada Park, tel. 028/7136-0880, www.museumoffreederry.org). Photos, shirts with bullet holes, and a video documentary convey Bogside residents' experiences during the worst of the Troubles. At the far end of the museum's outdoor wall (high up on the second floor of an adjacent residential building) is a copy of a famous painting by Francisco Goya depicting another massacre—this one in Spain—called the *Third of May 1808*. This reproduction draws a stark parallel to the local events that occurred here. Below and to the left of the painting (next to a gated alley) are two large bullet holes in the wall, inflicted on Bloody Sunday and preserved behind glass.

Cross over to the other side of Rossville Street to see the **Bloody Sunday Monument.** This small, fenced-off stone obelisk lists the names of those who died that day, most within 50 yards of this spot. Take a look at the map pedestal by the monument, which shows how a rubble barricade was erected to block the street. A 10-story housing project called Rossville Flats stood here in those days. After peaceful protests failed (with Bloody Sunday being the watershed event), Nationalist youths became more aggressive. British troops were wary of being hit by Molotov cocktails thrown from the rooftop of the housing project.

Cross back again, this time over to the grassy median strip that runs down the middle of Rossville Street. At this end stands a granite letter *H* inscribed with the names of the IRA hunger strikers who died (and how many days they starved) in the H-block of Maze Prison (see *"The Hunger Strikers,"* earlier in the walk).

Political Murals

The dramatic and emotional murals you'll encounter in Northern Ireland will likely be one of your trip's most enduring travel memories. During the 19th century, Protestant neighborhoods hung flags and streamers each July to commemorate the victory of King William of Orange at the Battle of the Boyne in 1690. Modern murals evolved from these colorful annual displays. With the advent of industrial paints, temporary seasonal displays became permanent territorial statements.

Unionist murals were created during the extended Home Rule political debate that eventually led to the partitioning of the island in 1921 and the creation of Northern Ireland. Murals that expressed opposing views in Nationalist Catholic neighborhoods were outlawed. The ban remained until the eruption of the modern Troubles, when staunchly Nationalist Catholic communities isolated themselves behind barricades, eluding state control and gaining freedom to express their pent-up passions. In Derry, this form of symbolic, cultural, and ideological resistance first appeared in 1969 with the simple "You are now entering Free Derry" message that you'll still see painted on the surviving gable wall at Free Derry Corner.

Found mostly in working-class neighborhoods of Belfast and Derry, today's political murals have become a dynamic form of popular culture. They blur the line between art and propaganda, giving visitors a striking glimpse of each community's history, identity, and values.

From here, as you look across at the corner of Fahan Street, you get a good view of two murals. In ❻ *The Runners* (right), four rioting youths flee tear gas from canisters used by the British Army to disperse hostile crowds. More than 1,000 canisters were used during the Battle of the Bogside; "nonlethal" rubber bullets killed 17 people over the course of the Troubles. Meanwhile, in ❼ *Operation Motorman* (left), a soldier wields a sledgehammer to break through a house door, depicting the massive push by the British Army to open up the Bogside's barricaded "no-go" areas that the IRA had controlled for three years (1969-1972).

Walk down to the other end of the median strip where the white wall of **Free Derry Corner** announces "You are now entering Free Derry" (imitating a similarly defiant slogan of the time in once-isolated West Berlin). This was the gabled end of a string of

houses that stood here almost 50 years ago. During the Troubles, it became a traditional meeting place for speakers to address crowds. A portion of this mural changes from time to time, calling attention to injustice suffered by kindred spirits around the world (the plight of Palestinians and Basques are common themes).

Cross back to the right side of the street (now Lecky Road) to see ❽ *Bloody Sunday,* in which a small group of men carry a body from that ill-fated march. It's based on a famous photo of Father Edward Daly that was taken that day. Hunched over, he waves a white handkerchief to request safe passage in order to evacuate a mortally wounded protester. The bloodstained civil rights banner was inserted under the soldier's feet for extra emphasis. After Bloody Sunday, the previously marginal IRA suddenly found itself swamped with bitterly determined young recruits.

Near it is a mural called ❾ *Bernadette.* The woman with the megaphone is Bernadette Devlin McAliskey, an outspoken civil rights leader, who, at age 21, became the youngest elected member of British Parliament. Behind her kneels a female supporter, banging a trash-can lid against the street in a traditional expression of protest in Nationalist neighborhoods. Trash-can lids were also used to warn neighbors of the approach of British patrols.

❿ *Petrol Bomber,* showing a teen wearing an army-surplus gas mask, captures the Battle of the Bogside, when locals barricaded their community, effectively shutting out British rule. Though the main figure's face is obscured by the mask, his body clearly communicates the resolve of an oppressed people. In the background, the long-gone Rossville Flats housing project still looms, with an Irish tricolor flag flying from its top.

In ⓫ *The Death of Innocence,* a young girl stands in front of bomb wreckage. She is Annette McGavigan, a 14-year-old who was killed on this corner by crossfire in 1971. She was the 100th fatality of the Troubles, which eventually took more than 3,000 lives (and she was also a cousin of one of the artists). The broken gun beside

her points to the ground, signifying that it's no longer being wielded. The large butterfly above her shoulder symbolizes the hope for peace. For years, the artists left the butterfly an empty silhouette until they felt confident that the peace process had succeeded. They finally filled in the butterfly with optimistic colors in the summer of 2006.

Finally, around the corner, you'll see a circle of male faces. This mural, painted in 1997 to observe the 25th anniversary of the tragedy, is called ⓬ *Bloody Sunday Commemoration* and shows the 14 victims. They are surrounded

by a ring of 14 oak leaves—the symbol of Derry. When relatives of the dead learned that the three Bogside Artists were beginning to paint this mural, many came forward to loan the artists precious photos of their loved ones, so they could be more accurately depicted.

Across the street, drop into the **Bogside Inn** for a beverage and check out the black-and-white photos of events in the area during the Troubles. This pub has been here through it all, and lives on to tell the tale.

While these murals preserve the struggles of the late 20th century, today sectarian violence has given way to negotiations and a settlement that seems to be working in fits and starts. The British apology for the Bloody Sunday shootings was a huge step forward. Former Nationalist leader John Hume (who shared the 1998 Nobel Peace Prize with then-Unionist leader David Trimble) once borrowed a quote from Gandhi to explain his nonviolent approach to the peace process: "An eye for an eye leaves everyone blind."

Sights in Derry

▲▲Tower Museum Derry

This well-organized museum combines modern audiovisual displays with historical artifacts to tell Derry's story from a skillfully unbiased viewpoint, sorting out some of the tangled history of Northern Ireland's Troubles. Occupying a modern reconstruction of a fortified medieval tower house that belonged to the local O'Doherty clan, it provides an excellent introduction to the city.

Cost and Hours: £4, includes audioguide for Armada exhibits, daily 10:00-17:30, last entry at 16:00, Union Hall Place, tel. 028/7137-2411, www.derrystrabane.com/towermuseum.

Visiting the Museum: The museum is divided into two sections: the Story of Derry (on the ground floor) and the Spanish Armada (on the four floors of the tower).

Start with the **Story of Derry,** which explains the city's monastic origins 1,500 years ago. The exhibit moves through pivotal events, such as the 1688-1689 siege, as well as unexpected blips, like Amelia Earhart's emergency landing. Don't miss the thought-provoking 15-minute film in the small theater—it offers an evenhanded local perspective on the tragic events of the modern sectarian conflict, giving you a better handle on what makes this unique city tick. Scan the displays of paramilitary paraphernalia in the hallway lined with colored curbstones—red, white, and blue Union Jack colors for Unionists; and the green, white, and orange Irish tricolor for Nationalists.

The tower section holds the **Spanish Armada** exhibits, filled with items taken from the wreck of *La Trinidad Valencera*. The ship sank off the coast of Donegal in 1588 in fierce storms nicknamed the "Protestant Winds." A third of the Armada's ships were lost in storms off the coasts of Ireland and Scotland. Survivors who made it ashore were hunted and killed by English soldiers. But a small number made it to Dunluce Castle (see page 53), where the sympathetic lord, who was no friend of the English, smuggled them to Scotland and eventual freedom in France.

Guildhall

This Neo-Gothic building, complete with clock tower, is the ceremonial seat of city government. Inside the hall are the Council Chamber, party offices, and an assembly hall featuring stained-glass windows showing scenes from Derry history.

Cost and Hours: Free, daily 10:00-17:30, free and clean WCs on ground floor, tel. 028/7137-6510, www.derrystrabane.com/guildhall.

Background: The Guildhall first opened in 1890 on reclaimed lands that were once the mudflats of the River Foyle. Destroyed by fire and rebuilt in 1913, it was massively damaged by IRA bombs in 1972. In an ironic twist, Gerry Doherty, one of those convicted of the bombings, was elected as a member of the Derry City Council a dozen years later. (When I first visited Derry with tour groups back in the 1990s, a bus of curious Americans was such a rarity that the mayor actually invited our entire group into his office here for tea and a friendly Q&A session.)

Visiting the Hall: Take an informational pamphlet from the front window and explore, if civic and cultural events are not taking place inside. Rotating exhibits fill a ground-floor hall just to the right of the front reception desk. The Ulster Plantation exhibition is worth a visit. A mighty pipe organ fills much of a wall in the grand hall. It's lonely and loves to be played (if you would like to give it a go, just ask a guard).

On the back terrace, facing the river, you'll find locals lunching at the pleasant Guild Café (daily 9:30-17:00). And across the street is the modest but heartfelt Peace Park, with hopeful, nonsectarian children's quotes on tiles that line the path.

Peace Bridge Stroll

Stroll across the architecturally fetching Peace Bridge for great views over the river toward the city center (best at sunset). The €14 million pedestrian Peace Bridge opened in 2011, linking neighborhoods long divided by the river (Catholic Nationalists on the west bank and Protestant Unionists on the east bank). On the far side from the old city walls, the former Ebrington Barracks British Army base (1841-2003) sits on prime real estate and surrounds a huge square that was once the military parade ground. This area features a fun gastropub, and serves as an outdoor concert venue and community gathering spot. Plans are in progress to develop this area further with a hotel and museum complex.

Hands Across the Divide

Designed by local teacher Maurice Harron, this powerful metal sculpture of two figures extending their hands to each other was inspired by the growing hope for peace and reconciliation in Northern Ireland (located at roundabout at west end of Craigavon Bridge).

The Tillie and Henderson's shirt factory (opened in 1857 and burned down in 2003) once stood on the banks of the river beside the bridge, looming over the figures. In its heyday, Derry's shirt industry employed more than 15,000 workers (90 percent of whom were women) in sweathouses typical of the human toll of the Industrial Revolution. Karl Marx mentioned this factory in *Das Kapital* as an example of women's transition from domestic to industrial work lives.

St. Columb's Cathedral

Marked by the tall spire inside the walls, this was the first Protestant cathedral built in Britain after the Reformation. St. Columb's played an important part in the defense of the city during the siege. During that time, cannons were mounted on its roof, and the original spire was scavenged for lead to melt into cannon shot. This Anglican cathedral was built from 1628 to 1633 in a style called "Planter's Gothic," financed by the same London companies that backed the Protestant plantation of Londonderry.

DERRY

Cost and Hours: £2 donation, Mon-Sat 9:00-17:00, closed Sun, tel. 028/7126-7313, www.stcolumbscathedral.org.

Visiting the Cathedral: Before you enter, walk over to the "Heroes' Mound" at the end of the churchyard closest to the town wall. Underneath this grassy dome is a mass grave of some of those who died during the 1689 siege.

In the cathedral entryway, you'll find a hollow cannonball that was lobbed into the city—it contained the besiegers' surrender terms. Inside, along the nave, hangs a musty collection of battle flags and Union Jacks that once inspired troops during the siege, the Crimean War, and World War II.

An American flag hung among them until a few years ago when its gradual deterioration prompted its current storage under glass (viewable in wooden case to right of front altar—fourth drawer from top). It's from the time when the first GIs to enter the European theater in World War II were based in Northern Ireland.

To the left of the front altar is a seven-minute video covering the cathedral's history. Check out the small chapter-house museum in the back of the church to see the huge original locks of the gates of Derry and more relics of the siege.

Long Tower Church

Built below the walls on the hillside above the Bogside, this modest-looking church is worth a visit for its stunning high altar. The name comes from a stone monastic round tower that stood here for centuries but was dismantled and used for building materials in the 1600s.

Cost and Hours: Free, generally open Mon-Sat 8:30-20:30, Sun 7:30-18:00, tel. 028/7126-2301, www.longtowerchurch.org.

Visiting the Church: Long Tower Church, the oldest Catholic church in Derry, was finished in 1786, during a time of enlightened relations between the city's two religious communities. Protestant Bishop Hervey gave a generous-for-the-time £200 donation and had the four Corinthian columns shipped in from Naples to frame the Neo-Renaissance altar.

Outside, walk behind the church and face the Bogside to find a simple shrine hidden beneath a hawthorn tree. It marks the spot where outlawed Masses were secretly held before this church was built, during the Penal Law period of the early 1700s. Through the Penal Laws, the English attempted to weaken Catholicism's influence by banishing priests and forbidding Catholics from buying land, attending school, voting, and holding office.

Nearby: The adjacent **St. Columba Heritage Centre** fleshes out the life of Derry's patron saint and founding father (£3, Mon-Fri 10:00-16:00, Sat-Sun from 13:00, closed Mon Oct-April, tel. 028/7136-8491, www.stcolumbscathedral.org).

Nightlife in Derry

The **Millennium Forum** is a modern venue that reflects the city's revived investment in local culture, concerts, and plays (box office open Mon-Sat 9:30-17:00, inside city walls on Newmarket Street near Ferryquay Gate, tel. 028/7126-4455, www.millenniumforum. co.uk, boxoffice@millenniumforum.co.uk).

The **Nerve Centre** hosts a wide variety of art-house films and live concerts (inside city walls at 7 Magazine Street, near Butcher Gate, tel. 028/7126-0562, www.nervecentre.org).

The **Playhouse Theatre** is an intimate venue for plays (£9-20 tickets, inside walls on Artillery Street, between New Gate and Ferryquay Gate, tel. 028/7126-8027, www.derryplayhouse.co.uk).

To mingle with Derry's friendly conversational residents, try **Peadar O'Donnell's** pub on Waterloo Street for the city's best nightly traditional music sessions (often start late, at 23:00; 53 Waterloo Street, tel. 028/7137-2318).

Sleeping in Derry

The first three options are located inside the city's walls and feature all the modern comforts. The others are in historic buildings with creaky charm and friendly hosts.

$$$$ Bishop's Gate Hotel is Derry's top lodging option and priced that way. A former gentlemen's club once frequented by Winston Churchill, it has 30 rooms that ooze with cushy refinement (fine bar, 24 Bishop Street, tel. 028/7114-0300, www.bishopsgatehotelderry.com, sales@bishopsgatehotelderry. com). They also rent one apartment (sleeps 4).

$$$$ The **Shipquay Hotel** rents 21 rooms with stylish minimalist comfort above its ground-floor Lock & Quay cocktail bar (15 Shipquay Street, tel. 028/7126-7266, www.shipquayhotel.com, info@shipquayhotel.com).

$$ Maldron Hotel features 93 modern and large rooms, a bistro restaurant, and 20 private basement parking spaces (Butcher

Street, tel. 028/7137-1000, www.maldronhotelderry.com, info. derry@maldronhotels.com).

$ Merchant's House, on a quiet street a 10-minute stroll from Waterloo Place, is a fine Georgian townhouse with a grand, colorful drawing room and nine rooms sporting marble fireplaces and ornate plasterwork (family rooms, 16 Queen Street, tel. 028/7126-9691, www.thesaddlershouse.com, saddlershouse@btinternet. com). Joan and Peter Pyne also run the Saddler's House (see below), and offer appealing self-catering townhouse rentals inside the walls (great for families or anyone needing extra space, 3-night minimum).

$ Saddler's House is a charming Victorian townhouse with seven rooms located a couple of blocks closer to the old town walls. Their muscular bulldog Bruno provides lovable comic relief (36 Great James Street, tel. 028/7126-9691, www.thesaddlershouse. com, saddlershouse@btinternet.com).

Eating in Derry

$$$ Entrada is a crisp, modern restaurant with a faintly Spanish theme, serving great meals and fine wines in a posh, calm space. It faces the river a block from the Guildhall (Wed-Sat 12:00-21:30, Sun until 20:00, closed Mon-Tue, Queens Quay, tel. 028/7137-3366).

The hip, trendy **$$$ Exchange Restaurant and Wine Bar** offers lunches and quality dinners with flair, in a central location near the river behind Waterloo Place (Mon-Fri 12:00-14:30 & 17:30-22:00, Sat 17:00-22:00, Sun 14:00-20:00, Queen's Quay, tel. 028/7127-3990).

$$$ Fitzroy's, tucked below Ferryquay Gate and stacked with locals, serves good lunches and dinners (Mon-Sat 12:00-22:00, Sun 13:00-20:00, 2 Bridge Street, tel. 028/7126-6211).

$$ Browns in Town is a casual, friendly lunch or dinner option near most of my recommended lodgings (Mon-Sat 12:00-15:00 & 17:30-21:00, Sun 17:00-20:30, 21 Strand Road, tel. 028/7136-2889).

$$ Walled City Brewery, across the Peace Bridge, is a fun change of pace. The brewpub ambience and dependable comfort food can be washed down with a local fave: Derry chocolate milk stout (Wed-Thu 17:00-23:30, Fri-Sun from 14:00, closed Mon-Tue, 70 Ebrington Square, tel. 028/7134-3336).

$ Mandarin Palace is crowded with loyal locals eating filling Chinese fare; easy takeout is available (Mon-Sat 16:00-23:00, Sun from 13:00, Queens Quay, tel. 028/7137-3656).

$ The Sandwich Company is a cheap and easy lunch counter and coffee shop in the center of the old town walls (Mon-Wed and

Sat 8:00-17:30, Thu-Fri until 19:00, Sun 10:00-17:00 (6 Bishop Street Within, tel. 028/7137-2500).

Supermarkets: You'll find everything you need for picnics at **Tesco** (Mon-Fri 8:00-21:00, Sat until 19:00, Sun 13:00-18:00, corner of Strand Road and Clarendon Street) or **SuperValu** (Mon-Sat 8:30-19:00, Sun 12:30-17:30, Waterloo Place).

Derry Connections

From Derry, it's an hour's drive to Portrush. If you're using public transportation, consider a Zone 4 iLink smartcard, good for all-day train and bus use in Northern Ireland (see page 63). Keep in mind that some bus and train schedules, road signs, and maps may say "Londonderry" or "L'Derry" instead of "Derry."

From Derry by Train to: Portrush (16/day, 1.5 hours, usually change in Coleraine), **Belfast** (16/day, 2 hours), **Dublin** (6/day, 4 hours, change in Belfast).

By Bus to: Galway (6/day, 5.5 hours), **Westport** (3/day, 6 hours, bus #64 to Knock Airport or Charleston then bus #440 to Derry), **Portrush** (5/day, 1.5 hours, change in Coleraine), **Belfast** (hourly, 2 hours), **Dublin** (12/day, 4 hours).

Near Derry

▲Ulster American Folk Park

This combination museum and folk park (in a wonderfully scenic and walkable rural forest) commemorates the many Irish who left their homeland during the hard times of the 18th century. Your visit progresses through four sections. You'll start by walking through the excellent museum, then head outdoors to visit the remaining three sections in chronological order: life in  Ulster before emigration, passage on the boat, and the adjustment to life in unfamiliar America. You'll gain insight into the origins of the tough Scots-Irish stock—think Davy Crockett (his people were from Derry) and Andrew Jackson (Carrickfergus roots)—who later shaped America's westward migration. You'll also find good coverage of the *Titanic* tragedy, and its effect on the Ulster folk who built the ship and the loved ones it left behind.

Cost and Hours: £9; Tue-Sun 10:00-17:00; Oct-Feb Tue-Fri

10:00-16:00, Sat-Sun from 11:00; closed Mon year-round; cafeteria, 2 Mellon Road, tel. 028/8224-3292, www.nmni.com.

Getting There: The folk park is 48 kilometers (30 miles) south of Derry on A-5—about a 45-minute drive.

Nearby: The adjacent **Mellon Centre for Migration Studies** is handy for genealogy searches (Tue-Fri 10:00-16:00, Sat from 11:00, closed Sun-Mon, tel. 028/8225-6315, www.qub.ac.uk/cms).

PORTRUSH & THE ANTRIM COAST

The Antrim Coast—the north of Northern Ireland—is one of the most interesting and scenic coastlines in Ireland. Portrush, at the end of the train line, is an ideal base for exploring the highlights of the Antrim Coast. Within a few miles of the train terminal, you can visit evocative castle ruins, tour the world's oldest whiskey distillery, catch a thrill on a bouncy rope bridge, and hike along the famous Giant's Causeway.

PLANNING YOUR TIME

You need a full day to explore the Antrim Coast, so allow two nights in Portrush. The main sights on the coast are the Giant's Causeway, Old Bushmills Distillery, Carrick-a-Rede Rope Bridge, and Dunluce Castle (all doable with a car in one busy day). Add a third night if you plan to take longer hikes and visit Rathlin Island (book ahead for summer ferries).

Advance planning is important here. Book a timed-entry ticket online to cross the Carrick-a-Rede Rope Bridge. Arrive early for the Giant's Causeway (a guided hike can be booked a day in advance; can also be done on your own with no reservation). For sights that can't be reserved, pick the one that most interests you and visit it first, then take your chances with the rest. Visit Dunluce Castle last; it's the least crowded of these four main choices.

Getting an early start is essential. My ideal day would start with the Giant's Causeway, arriving by 9:00, when crowds are lightest—choose between a quickie visit or longer hike (options described on page 47). Early birds will find that the trails are always open.

Follow this with a tour of Old Bushmills Distillery. For lunch, you can bring a picnic, or eat cheaply in either the visitors center at the causeway or the Old Bushmills hospitality room.

After lunch, drive to Carrick-a-Rede (about 20 minutes from the distillery). Without a ticket, you can still enjoy the scenic cliff-top trail hike all the way to the bridge, as well as the nearby viewpoint for dramatic views of the bridge.

From here, hop in your car and double back west all the way to dramatically cliff-perched Dunluce Castle for a late-afternoon tour. The castle is only a five-minute drive from Portrush.

If driving on to Belfast from Portrush, consider the slower but scenic coastal route via the Glens of Antrim.

GETTING AROUND THE ANTRIM COAST

By Car: A car is the best way to explore the charms of the Antrim Coast. Distances are short and parking is easy.

By Bus: In peak season, an all-day bus pass helps you get around the region economically. The **Causeway Rambler** links Portrush to Old Bushmills Distillery, the Giant's Causeway, and the Carrick-a-Rede Rope Bridge (stopping at the nearby town of Ballintoy). The bus journey from Portrush to Carrick-a-Rede takes 45 minutes (£7.50/day, runs roughly 10:00-18:00, hourly May-Sept, fewer off-season). Pick up a Rambler bus schedule at the TI, and buy the ticket from the driver (in Portrush, the Rambler stops at Dunluce Avenue, next to public WC, a 2-minute walk from TI; operated by Translink, tel. 028/9066-6630, www.translink.co.uk).

By Bus Tour: If you're based in Belfast, you can visit most of the sights on the Antrim Coast with a **McComb's** tour (see page 65). Those based in Derry can get to the Giant's Causeway and Carrick-a-Rede Rope Bridge with City Sightseeing (see page 17).

By Taxi: Groups (up to four) can reasonably visit most sights by taxi (except the more distant Carrick-a-Rede and Rathlin Island sailings from Ballycastle). Approximate one-way prices from Portrush: £12 (Dunluce Castle), £15 (Old Bushmills Distillery), £23 (Giant's Causeway). Try **Andy Brown's Taxi** (tel. 028/7082-2223), **Hugh's Taxi** (mobile 077-0298-6110), or **North West Taxi** (tel. 028/7082-4446).

Portrush

Homey Portrush used to be known as "the Brighton of the North." It first became a resort in the late 1800s, as railroads expanded to offer the new middle class a weekend by the shore. Victorians believed that swimming in saltwater would cure many common ailments.

This is County Antrim, the Bible Belt of Northern Ireland. When a large supermarket chain decided to stay open on Sundays, a local reverend called for a boycott of the store for not honoring the Sabbath. And in 2012, when the Giant's Causeway Visitor Centre opened, local Creationists demanded that, alongside modern geologic explanations about the age of the unique rock formations, an exhibit be added explaining their viewpoint (that, according to the Bible, the earth here was only 6,000 years old, not 60 million—carbon dating be damned).

While it's seen its best days, Portrush retains the atmosphere and architecture of a genteel seaside resort. Its peninsula is filled with lowbrow, family-oriented amusements, fun eateries, and B&Bs. Summertime fun seekers promenade along the tiny harbor and tumble down to the sandy beaches, which extend in sweeping white crescents on either side.

Superficially, Portrush has the appearance of any small British seaside resort (and Union Jacks fly with a little extra gusto around here), but its history and large population of young people (students from nearby University of Ulster at Coleraine) give the town a little more personality. Along with the usual arcade amusements, there are nightclubs, restaurants, summer theater productions in the Town Hall, and convivial pubs that attract customers all the way from Belfast.

Orientation to Portrush

Portrush's pleasant and easily walkable town center features sea views in every direction. On one side are the harbor and most of the restaurants, and on the other are Victorian townhouses and vast, salty vistas. The tip of the peninsula is filled with tennis courts, lawn-bowling greens, putting greens, and a park.

The town is busy with students during the school year. July and August are beach-resort boom time. June and September are laid-back and lazy. There's a brief but intense spike in visitors in mid-May for a huge annual motorcycle race and on Easter weekend (see "Crowd Alert" later). Families pack Portrush on Saturdays, and revelers from Belfast crowd its hotels on Saturday nights.

Tourist Information: The TI is located underneath the very central, red-brick Town Hall (Mon-Sat 9:00-17:00, Sun 11:00-16:00, shorter hours off-season and closed Oct-March; Kerr Street, tel. 028/7082-3333). Consider the Collins Ireland Visitors Map (£9), the free *Visitor Guide* brochure, and, if needed, a free Belfast map.

Arrival in Portrush: The train tracks stop at the base of the tiny peninsula that Portrush fills (no baggage storage at station). Most of my listed B&Bs are within a 10-minute walk of the train station. The bus stop is two blocks from the train station.

Crowd Alert: Over a four-day weekend in mid-May, thousands of die-hard motorcycle fans converge on Portrush, Port Stewart, and Coleraine to watch the **Northwest 200 Race.** Fearless racers scorch the roads at 200 miles per hour on the longest straightaway in motorsports. Accommodations fill up a year ahead, and traffic is the pits (dates and details at www.northwest200.org). Avoid visiting during crowded **Easter weekend.**

Laundry: Full service is available at **Causeway Laundry** (Mon-Tue and Thu-Fri 9:00-16:30, Wed and Sat until 13:00, closed Sun, 68 Causeway Street, tel. 028/7082-2060).

Sights in Portrush

Barry's Old Time Amusement Arcade

This fun arcade is bigger than it looks and offers a chance to see Northern Ireland at play. Older locals visit for the nostalgia as many of the rides and amusements go back 50 years. Ride prices are listed at the door. Everything runs with tokens (£0.50 each or £10/24, buy from coin-op machines). Located just below the train station on the harbor, Barry's is filled with "candy floss" (cotton candy) and crazy "scoop treats" (daily 12:30-22:00 in summer, weekends only Easter-May, closed Sept-Easter, www.barrysamusements.com).

Royal Portrush Golf Club

Irish courses, like those in Scotland, are highly sought after for their lush greens in glorious settings. Serious golfers can get a tee time at the Royal Portrush, a links course that hosted the British Open in 1951 and then again in 2019. Check out the trophy case and historic photos in the clubhouse (green fees generally £220, less most days in off-season). The adjacent, slightly shorter Valley Course is more budget-friendly (green fees £50, 10-minute walk from station, tel. 028/7082-2311, www.royalportrushgolfclub.com).

Portrush Recreation Grounds

For some easygoing exercise right in town, this well-organized park offers lawn-bowling greens (£6/hour with gear), putting greens, tennis courts, and a great kids' play park. You can rent tennis shoes, balls, and rackets, all for £10/hour (Mon-Sat 10:00-dusk, Sun from 12:00, closed mid-Sept-May, tel. 028/7082-4441).

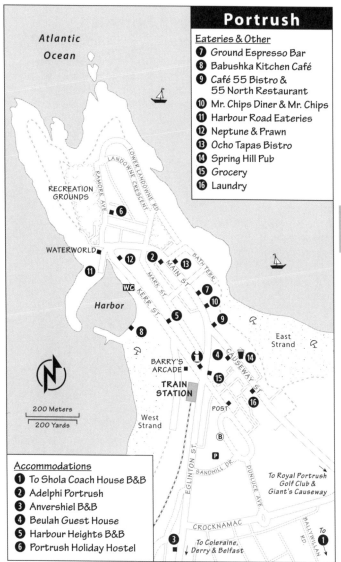

PORTRUSH & ANTRIM COAST

Waterworld

For more fun, consider Waterworld, with pools, waterslides, and bowling (£5, Mon-Sat 10:30-18:00, Sun from 12:00, closed Sept-June; wedged between Harbour Bistro and Ramore Wine Bar overlooking the harbor, tel. 028/7082-2001).

Sleeping in Portrush

Portrush's hotels range from depressing to ritzy. Some B&Bs are well worn. August and Saturday nights can be crowded (and loud) with young party groups. Otherwise, it's a "you take half a loaf when you can get it" town. Sea views are worth paying for only if you get a bay window. Ask for a big room (some doubles can be very small; twins are bigger). Lounges are invariably grand and have bay-window views. Most places listed have lots of stairs. Parking is easy.

$$$ Shola Coach House is a memorable treat that exceeds other B&B experiences in Northern Ireland. About 1.5 miles south of town, it's easiest for drivers (otherwise it's a 30-minute uphill walk or £5 taxi ride). The secluded, 170-year-old, renovated stone structure once housed the coaches and horses for a local landlord. The decor of the four rooms is tasteful, the garden patio is delightful, and Sharon and David Schindler keep it spotless (parking, no kids under 18, 2-night minimum, 110A Gateside Road at top of Ballywillan Road, tel. 028/7082-5925, mobile 075-6542-7738, www.sholabandb.com, sholabandb@gmail.com).

$$$ Adelphi Portrush is the best large hotel in town, with 28 tastefully furnished modern rooms, an ideal location, and a hearty bistro downstairs (family rooms, 67 Main Street, tel. 028/7082-5544, www.adelphiportrush.com, stay@adelphiportrush.com).

$ Anvershiel B&B, with seven nicely refurbished rooms, is a great value (RS%, family rooms, parking, 10-minute walk south of train station, 16 Coleraine Road, tel. 028/7082-3861, www.anvershiel.com, enquiries@anvershiel.com, Alan and Janice Thompson).

$ Beulah Guest House is a traditional, old-fashioned place. It's centrally located and run by cheerful Helen and Charlene McLaughlin, with 11 prim rooms (parking at rear, 16 Causeway Street, tel. 028/7082-2413, www.beulahguesthouse.com, stay@beulahguesthouse.com).

$ Harbour Heights B&B rents nine retro-homey rooms, each named after a different town in County Antrim. It has an inviting guest lounge, supervised by two tabby cats, overlooking the harbor. Friendly South African hosts Sam and Tim Swart, a photographer, manage the place with a light hand (family rooms, 17 Kerr Street, tel. 028/7082-2765, mobile 078-9586-6534, www.harbourheightsportrush.com, info@harbourheightsportrush.com).

¢ Portrush Holiday Hostel offers clean, well-organized, economical lodging (private rooms available, tel. 028/7082-1288, mobile 078-5037-7367, 24 Princess Street, www.portrushholidayhostel.com, portrushholidayhostel@gmail.com).

Eating in Portrush

As a family getaway from Belfast and a beach escape for students from the nearby university in Coleraine, Portrush has more than enough fish-and-chips joints. And in recent years, the refined tastes of affluent golfers and urban professionals out for a weekend has prompted the town to up its culinary game.

LUNCH SPOTS

$ Ground Espresso Bar makes fresh sandwiches and panini, soup, and great coffee (daily 9:00-17:00, July-Aug until 22:00, 52 Main Street, tel. 028/7082-5979).

$ Babushka Kitchen Café serves fresh sandwiches and creative desserts with an unbeatable view—actually out on the pier (daily 9:15-17:00, West Strand Promenade, tel. 077-8750-2012).

$$ Café 55 Bistro serves basic sandwiches with a great patio view (daily 9:00-17:00, longer hours in summer, shorter hours off-season, 1 Causeway Street, beneath fancier 55 North restaurant, tel. 028/7082-2811).

$ Mr. Chips Diner and **Mr. Chips** are the local favorites for cheap, quality fish-and-chips (daily 12:00-22:00, 12 and 20 Main Street). Both are mostly takeout while the diner also has tables. The smaller Mr. Chips cooks with lard (less healthy, more traditional). The bigger Mr. Chips cooks with vegetable oil (healthier) and hangs the stars and bars of the Confederate flag on the wall (when it comes to the Catholic/Protestant issue, this is a conservative town with some redneck tendencies).

Groceries: For picnic supplies, try **Spar Market** (daily 7:00-20:00, summer until 23:00, across from Barry's Arcade on Main Street, tel. 028/7082-5447).

HARBOUR ROAD EATERIES

A creative, diverse, and lively cluster of restaurants overlooks the harbor. With the same owner, they all have a creative and fun energy, are often jammed with diners, and are basically open from about 17:00 to 22:00. All are described at RamoreRestaurant.com. Only Basalt and Mermaid Kitchen & Bar take reservations.

$$ Ramore Wine Bar is a salty, modern place, with an inviting menu ranging from steaks to vegetarian items. It's very casual but with serious cuisine. Order at the bar and take a table (open daily for lunch and dinner, tel. 028/7082-4313).

$$ The Tourist is a hit for its pizza, tacos, burritos, and burgers. It's noisy and youthful with tight seating (daily, tel. 028/7082-3311).

$$$ Harbour Bistro is dark, noisy, and sprawling with a sloppy crowd enjoying chargrilled meat and fish (daily, no kids after 20:00, tel. 028/7082-2430).

$$ Mermaid Kitchen & Bar is all about fresh fish dishes with a Spanish twist and great harbor views. Those at the bar get a bird's-eye view of the fun banter and precision teamwork of the kitchen staff (closed Mon-Tue, no kids under 18, tel. 028/7082-6969).

$$ Basalt has Spanish-influenced small plates and an outdoor terrace (closed Wed-Thu, no kids under 18, tel. 028/7082-6969).

$$$ Neptune & Prawn (just across the inlet from the others) is the most yacht-clubby of the bunch. Serving Asian and other international food, with a fancy presentation and many plates designed to be shared, this place is noisy and high-energy, with rock music playing (daily, no kids under 18, tel. 028/7082-2448).

OTHER DINING OPTIONS OFF THE HARBOR

$$$ 55 North (named for the local latitude) has the best sea views in town, with windows on three sides. The filling pasta-and-fish dishes, along with some Asian plates, are a joy. Their lunch and early-bird special (order by 18:45) is three courses at the cost of the entrée (daily 12:30-14:00 & 17:00-21:00, 1 Causeway Street, tel. 028/7082-2811).

$$ Ocho Tapas Bistro brings sunny Spanish cuisine to the chilly north, featuring a great early-bird menu—choose any three tapas from a varied list (Tue-Fri 17:00-21:30, Sat-Sun 12:30-14:30 & 17:00-22:00, closed Mon, 92 Main Street, tel. 028/7082-4110).

PUBS

Harbour Bar is an old-fashioned pub next to the Harbour Bistro (see above). **Harbour Gin Bar** (above Harbour Bar) is romantic and classy—a rustic, spacious, and inviting place with live acoustic folk music from 20:30 (almost nightly) and a fun selection of 45 gins.

Neptune & Prawn Cocktail Bar (above the restaurant by the same name; see listing above) has great views over the harbor and is the most classy-yet-inviting place in town for a drink.

Spring Hill Pub is a good bet for its friendly vibe and occasional live music, including traditional sessions Thursdays at 21:30 (17 Causeway Street, tel. 028/7082-3361).

Portrush Connections

Consider a £17.50 Zone 4 iLink smartcard, good for all-day Translink train and bus use in Northern Ireland (£16.50 top-up for each additional day). Translink's website has the latest schedules and prices for both trains and buses in Northern Ireland (tel. 028/9066-6630, www.translink.co.uk).

From Portrush by Train to: Coleraine (hourly, 12 minutes), **Belfast** (15/day, 2 hours, transfer in Coleraine), **Dublin** (7/day, 5 hours, transfer in Belfast). Note that on Sundays, service is greatly reduced.

By Bus to: Belfast (12/day, 2 hours; scenic coastal route, 2.5 hours), **Dublin** (4/day, 5.5 hours).

Antrim Coast

The craggy 20-mile stretch of the Antrim Coast extending eastward from Portrush to Ballycastle rates second only to the tip of the Dingle Peninsula as the prettiest chunk of coastal Ireland. From your base in Portrush, you have a grab bag of sightseeing choices: Giant's Causeway, Old Bushmills Distillery, Dunluce Castle, Carrick-a-Rede Rope Bridge, and Rathlin Island.

It's easy to weave these sights together by car, but connections are patchy by public transportation. Bus service is viable only in summer, and taxi fares are reasonable only for the sights closest to Portrush (Dunluce Castle, Old Bushmills Distillery, and the Giant's Causeway). For details on how to plan your day on the Antrim Coast, and for more on your transportation options, see "Planning Your Time" and "Getting Around the Antrim Coast," at the beginning of this chapter.

The Scottish Connection

The Romans called the Irish the "Scoti" (meaning pirates). When the Scoti crossed the narrow Irish Sea and invaded the land of the Picts 1,500 years ago, that region became known as Scoti-land. Ireland and Scotland were never conquered by the Romans, and they retained similar clannish Celtic traits. Both share the same Gaelic branch of the linguistic tree.

On clear summer days from Carrick-a-Rede, the island of Mull in Scotland—only 17 miles away—is visible. Much closer on the horizon is the boomerang-shaped Rathlin Island, part of Northern Ireland. Rathlin is where Scottish leader Robert the Bruce (a compatriot of William "Braveheart" Wallace) retreated in 1307 after defeat at the hands of the English. Legend has it that he hid in a cave on the island, where he observed a spider patiently rebuilding its web each time a breeze knocked it down. Inspired by the spider's perseverance, Robert gathered his Scottish forces once more and finally defeated the English at the decisive Battle of Bannockburn.

Flush with confidence from his victory, Robert the Bruce decided to open a second front against the English...in Ireland. In 1315, he sent his brother Edward over to enlist their Celtic Irish cousins in an effort to thwart the English. After securing Ireland, Edward hoped to move on and enlist the Welsh, thus cornering England with their pan-Celtic nation. But Edward's timing was bad—Ireland was in the midst of famine. His Scottish troops had to live off the land and began to take food and supplies from the starving Irish. He might also have been trying to destroy Ireland's crops to keep them from being used as a colonial "breadbasket" to feed English troops. The Scots quickly wore out their welcome, and Edward the Bruce was eventually killed in battle near Dundalk in 1318.

This was the first time in history that Ireland was used as a pawn by England's enemies. Spain and France saw Ireland as the English Achilles' heel, and both countries later attempted invasions of the island. The English Tudor and Stuart royalty countered these threats in the 16th and 17th centuries by starting the "plantation" of loyal subjects in Ireland. The only successful long-term settlement by the English was here in Northern Ireland, which remains part of the United Kingdom today.

It's interesting to imagine how things might be different today if Ireland and Scotland had been permanently welded together as a nation 700 years ago. You'll notice the strong Scottish influence in this part of Ireland when you ask a local a question and he answers, "Aye, a wee bit." The Irish joke that the Scots are just Irish people who couldn't swim home.

Sights on the Antrim Coast

▲▲Giant's Causeway

This five-mile-long stretch of coastline is famous for its bizarre basalt columns. The shore is covered with largely hexagonal pillars that stick up at various heights. It's as if the earth were offering God a choice of 37,000 six-sided cigarettes.

Geologists claim the Giant's Causeway was formed by volcanic eruptions more than 60 million years ago. As the surface of the lava flow quickly cooled, it contracted and crystallized into columns (resembling the caked mud at the bottom of a dried-up lakebed, but with far deeper cracks). As the rock later settled and eroded, the columns broke off into the many stair-like steps that now honeycomb the Antrim Coast.

Of course, in actuality, the Giant's Causeway was made by a giant Ulster warrior named Finn MacCool who knew of a rival giant living across the water in Scotland. Finn built a stone bridge over to Scotland to spy on his rival, and found out that the Scottish giant was much bigger. Finn retreated back to Ireland and had his wife dress him as a sleeping infant, just in time for the rival giant to come across the causeway to spy on Finn. The rival, shocked at the infant's size, fled back to Scotland in terror of whomever had sired this giant baby. Breathing a sigh of relief, Finn tore off the baby clothes and prudently knocked down the bridge. Today, proof of this encounter exists in the geologic formation that still extends undersea and surfaces in Scotland (at the island of Staffa).

Cost and Hours: The Giant's Causeway is free and always open. But in practice, anyone parking there needs to pay £12.50/adult. This includes an audioguide (or one-hour guided walk; leaves regularly with demand), a map, and entrance to the visitors center (daily 9:00-18:00, June-Sept until 19:00, Nov-March until 17:00, tel. 028/2073-1855, www.nationaltrust.org.uk/giantscauseway). A gift shop and café are in the visitors center.

Visiting the Causeway: For cute variations on the Finn story, as well as details on the ridiculous theories of modern geologists, start in the **Giant's Causeway Visitor Centre.** It's filled with kid-friendly interactive exhibits giving a worthwhile history of the Giant's Causeway, with a regional overview. On the far wall opposite the entrance, check out the interesting three-minute video showing the evolution of the causeway from molten lava to the geometric,

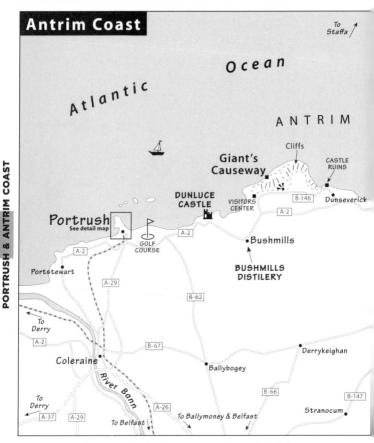

geologic wonderland of today. The large 3-D model of the causeway offers a bird's-eye view of the region. There's also an exhibit about the history of tourism here from the 18th century.

The **causeway** itself is the highlight of the entire coast. The audioguide highlights 15 stops along the causeway, each with a photo of the formation being described; all stops are shown on the map you'll receive with your ticket.

From the visitors center, you have several options for visiting the causeway:

Short and Easy: A **shuttle bus** (4/hour from 9:00, £1 each way) zips tourists a half-mile from the visitors center down a paved road to the causeway. This standard route (the blue dashed line on your map) offers the easiest access and follows the stops on your audioguide. Many choose to walk down and then take the shuttle back up.

Mid-Level Hike: For a longer hike and a more varied dose of causeway views, consider the cliff-top trail (red dashed line on

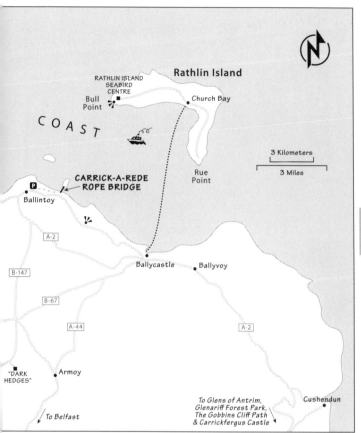

your map). Take the easy-to-follow trail uphill from the visitors center 10 minutes to Weir's Snout, the great fence-protected preci-

pice viewpoint. Then hike 15 minutes farther (level) to reach the Shepherd's Steps. Then grab the banister on the steep (and slippery-when-wet) stairs that zigzag down the switchbacks toward the water. At the T-junction, go 100 yards right, to the towering rock pipes of "the Organ." (You can detour another 500 yards east around the headland, but the trail dead-ends there.) Now retrace your steps west on the trail (don't go up the steps again), continuing down to the tidal zone, where the "Giant's Boot" (6-foot boulder, on the right) provides some photo fun. Another 100 yards

For *Game of Thrones* Fans

Even if you don't give a bloody Stark about the *Game of Thrones* TV saga, you'll notice references to it as you travel around Northern Ireland. Much of the series was filmed here, both on location and in the Titanic Quarter studio in Belfast. An average visit to the Antrim Coast is a traipse through the set: Dragonstone, the Stormlands, and the Iron Islands were brought to life along the same route that travelers use to see Dunluce Castle and Carrick-a-Rede Rope Bridge. For those who are truly interested in the approach of a very long winter, there are several options: both McComb's (www.mccombscoaches.com; see page 65) and Game of Thrones Tours (www.gameofthronestours.com) run day tours from Belfast or Derry to various spots in the seven kingdoms.

With a car, use the map at www.discovernorthernireland.com/GameofThrones to find filming locations. Without leaving County Antrim, you can visit Ballintoy Harbour (Stormlands), Larrybane (Iron Islands), Murlough Bay (Storm's End), and the Dark Hedges (King's Road) with no more than an hour's driving time. Just avoid any reenactments, as the nearest major hospital that treats dragon burns is in Belfast.

farther is the dramatic point where the causeway meets the sea. Just beyond that, at the asphalt turnaround, is the shuttle bus stop.

Just below the bus stop is a fine place to explore the uneven, wave-splashed rock terraces, watching your every easy-to-trip step. Look for "wishing coins"—rusted and bent—that have been jammed into the cracks of rock just behind the turnaround (where the trail passes through a notch in the 20-foot-high rock wall).

Return to the visitors center by hiking up the paved lane (listening to the audioguide at stops along the way). Or, from the turnaround, you can catch the shuttle bus back to the visitors center (just line up and pay the driver).

Longer Hike: Hardy hikers and avid photographers can join the guided **Clifftop Experience** trek exploring the trail that runs along a five-mile section of the Causeway Coast, starting at the meager ruins of Dunseverick Castle—east of Giant's Causeway on B-146 (yellow dashed line on your map). The hike is led by a naturalist, who ventures beyond the usual big-bus tourist crowds to explore the rugged rim of this most-scenic section of the Antrim Coast. Expect undulating grass and gravel paths with no WC options and no shelter whatsoever from bad weather (£35, includes parking; daily at 12:15, Nov-Feb at 10:15, must book online by 16:00 a day ahead; allow 3.5 hours, no kids under 12, hikers meet at visitors center and bus to Dunseverick trailhead, tel. 028/2073-

3419, www.giantscausewaytickets.com, northcoastbookings@nationaltrust.org.uk).

The Clifftop Experience hike route is a public right-of-way and can also be done on your own. If going independently, a good plan is to take the Causeway Rambler bus (see "Getting Around the Antrim Coast," earlier) or a taxi from Portrush to Dunseverick Castle and hike to the visitors center (there's also limited parking at the Dunseverick Castle trailhead). From the castle, hike west, following the cliff-hugging contours of Benbane Head back to the visitors center. You'll generally have a fence on your left and the cliff on the right, so there's little doubt about the route. When you reach the visitors center, it's easy to arrange travel back to Portrush by taxi or Rambler bus (check bus schedules ahead of time at Portrush TI or at www.translink.co.uk). For more info on hiking the route without a naturalist, see www.visitcausewaycoastandglens.com and search for "North Antrim Cliff Path." Note that occasional rock falls and slides can close this trail (ask first at Portrush TI, or call ahead to visitors center).

▲▲Old Bushmills Distillery

Bushmills claims to be the world's oldest distillery. Though King James I (of Bible translation fame) only granted Bushmills its license to distill "Aqua Vitae" in 1608, whiskey has been made here since the 13th century. Distillery tours waft you through the process, making it clear that Irish whiskey is triple distilled—and therefore smoother than Scotch whisky (distilled merely twice).

Cost and Hours: £9 for 45-minute tour followed by a tasting; tours go on the half-hour Mon-Sat 9:30-16:00 (last tour), Sun from 12:00; Nov-March tours run Mon-Sat 10:00-15:30 (last tour), Sun from 12:00; tours are limited to 18 people and can fill up (only groups of 15 or more can reserve ahead); note that in July, you can still tour, but the distillery machinery is shut down for annual maintenance; tel. 028/2073-3218, www.bushmills.com.

Visiting the Distillery: Tours start with the mash pit, which is filled with a porridge that eventually becomes whiskey. (The leftovers of that porridge are fed to the county's particularly happy cows.) Bushmills is made of only three ingredients: malted barley, water, and yeast. You'll see a huge room full of whiskey aging in oak casks—casks already used to make bourbon, sherry, and port.

Whiskey picks up its color and personality from this wood (which breathes and has an effective life of 30 years). Bushmills shapes the flavor of its whiskey by carefully finessing the aging process—often in a mix of these casks.

To see the distillery at its lively best, visit when the 100 workers are staffing the machinery—Monday morning through Friday noon. (The still is still on weekends and in July.) The finale, of course, is the opportunity for a sip in the 1608 Bar—the former malt barn. Visitors get a single glass of their choice. Hot-drink enthusiasts might enjoy a cinnamon-and-cloves hot toddy. Teetotalers can just order tea. After the tour, you can get a decent lunch in the hospitality room.

Shoppers: The distillery cannot ship purchases. See their website for details on bringing alcohol back home in your luggage.

Nearby: The distillery is just outside of **Bushmills town,** which is a Unionist festival of red, white, and blue flags and bunting. Banners posted throughout the town celebrate illustrious Ulster men and women and people far and wide with Ulster heritage (like Mark Twain and Dolly Parton).

▲▲Carrick-a-Rede Rope Bridge

For 200 years, fishermen hung a narrow, 90-foot-high bridge (planks strung between wires) across a 65-foot-wide chasm between the mainland and a tiny island. Today, the bridge (while not the original version) gives access to the sea stack where salmon nets were set (until 2002) during summer months to catch the fish turning and hugging the coast's corner. (The complicated system is described at the gateway.) A pleasant, 30-minute, one-mile

walk from the parking lot takes you down to the rope bridge. Cross over to the island for fine views and great seabird-watching, especially during nesting season. A coffee shop and WCs are near the parking lot.

Cost and Hours: £9 trail and bridge fee, book online in advance; daily 9:30-18:00, June-Aug until 20:00, Nov-Feb until 15:30, last entry 45 minutes before closing; tel. 028/2076-9839, www.nationaltrust.org.uk.

Advance Tickets Recommended: Tickets sell out and lines can be long. Buying a timed-entry ticket in advance will save you time and possibly the frustration of not getting a ticket at all (available at http://carrickaredetickets.com; can sell out up to 4 months in advance). Without an advance ticket, arrive as early as possible.

Nearby Viewpoint: If you have a car and a picnic lunch, don't miss the terrific coastal scenic rest area one mile steeply uphill and east of Carrick-a-Rede (on B-15 to Ballycastle). This grassy area offers one of the best picnic views in Northern Ireland (tables but no WCs). Feast on bird's-eye views of the rope bridge, nearby Rathlin Island, and the not-so-distant Island of Mull in Scotland.

▲Dunluce Castle

These romantic ruins, perched dramatically on the edge of a rocky headland, are a testimony to this region's turbulent past. During the Middle Ages, the castle was a prized fortification. But on a stormy night in 1639, dinner was interrupted as half of the kitchen fell into the sea, taking the servants with it. That was the last straw for the lady of the castle. The countess of Antrim packed

up and moved inland, and the castle "began its slow submission to the forces of nature."

Cost and Hours: £5.50, daily 10:00-17:00, winter until 16:00, tel. 028/2073-1938.

Visiting the Castle: While it's one of the largest castles in Northern Ireland and is beautifully situated, there's precious little left to see among Dunluce's broken walls. Look for distinctively hexagonal stones embedded in the castle walls, plucked straight from the unique pillars of rock making up the nearby Giant's Causeway.

Before entering, catch the eight-minute video about the history of the castle (across from the ticket desk). The ruins themselves are dotted with plaques that show interesting artists' renditions of how the place would have looked 400 years ago.

There were primitive fortifications here hundreds of years before the castle was built. Your guide will point out the underground hiding place where locals would try to wait out Viking raiders. But the 16th century saw the most expansion of the castle and was financed by treasure salvaged from a shipwreck. In 1588, the Spanish Armada's *Girona*—overloaded with sailors and the valuables of three abandoned sister ships—sank on her way home after the aborted mission against England. More than 1,300 drowned, and only five survivors washed ashore. The shipwreck was more fully excavated in 1967, and a bounty of golden odds and silver ends wound up in Belfast's Ulster Museum.

Rathlin Island

The only inhabited island off the coast of Northern Ireland, Rathlin is a quiet haven for hikers, birdwatchers, and seal spotters. Less than seven miles from end to end, this "L"-shaped island is reachable by ferry from the town of Ballycastle.

Getting There: The Rathlin Island passenger-only ferry departs from Ballycastle, just east of Carrick-a-Rede. There are 11 trips per day in summer: seven fast 30-minute trips, and four slower one-hour trips (£12 round-trip per passenger, smart to book ahead, as the ferry can sell out on summer days; tel. 028/2076-9299, www.rathlinballycastleferry.com).

Drivers can park in Ballycastle (only special-permit holders can take a car onto the ferry). A taxi from Portrush to Ballycastle runs £30 one-way. Bus service from Portrush to Ballycastle is spotty (check with the TI in Portrush, or contact Translink—tel. 028/9066-6630, www.translink.co.uk).

Visiting Rathlin Island: Rathlin's population of 110 islanders clusters around the ferry dock at Church Bay. Here you'll find the **Rathlin Boathouse Visitor Centre,** which operates as the island's TI (daily 10:00-12:30 & 13:00-17:00, closed in winter, on the bay 100 yards east of the ferry dock, tel. 028/2076-0054).

In summer, a shuttle bus (£5 round-trip) meets arriving ferries and drives visitors to the **Rathlin Island Seabird Centre** at the west end of the island. Entry to the Seabird Centre includes a tour of its unique lighthouse, extending down the cliff with its beacon at the bottom (£5, daily 10:00-16:00, May-Aug until 17:00, closed Oct-Feb). It's upside-down because the coast guard wants the light visible only from a certain distance out to sea. The bird observation terrace at the center (next to the lighthouse) overlooks one of the most dramatic coastal views in Ireland—a sheer drop of more than 300 feet to craggy sea stacks just offshore that are draped in thousands of seabirds. Bring your most powerful zoom lens for photos.

Rathlin has seen its fair share of history. Flint ax heads were quarried here in Neolithic times. The island was one of the first in Ireland to be raided by Vikings, in 795. Robert the Bruce hid out from English pursuers on Rathlin in the early 1300s (see "The Scottish Connection" sidebar, earlier). In the late 1500s, local warlord Sorely Boy MacDonnell stashed his extended family on Rathlin and waited on the mainland at Dunluce Castle to face his English enemies...only to watch in horror as they headed for the island instead to massacre his loved ones. And in 1917, a WWI U-boat sank the British cruiser HMS *Drake* in Church Bay. The wreck is now a popular scuba-dive destination, 60 feet below the surface.

▲Antrim Mountains and Glens

Not particularly high (never more than 1,500 feet), the Antrim Mountains are cut by a series of large glens running northeast to the sea. Glenariff, with its waterfalls—especially the Mare's Tail—is the most beautiful of the nine glens (described next). Travelers going by car can take a pleasant drive from Portrush to Belfast, sticking to the (more scenic but less direct) A-2 road that stays near the coast and takes in parts of all the Glens of Antrim.

▲Glenariff Forest Park

Glenariff Forest Park offers scenic picnic spots and lush hiking trails as well as a cozy tea shop. The parking lot alone has a lovely view down the glen to the sea. You'll find more spectacular scenery on the three-mile waterfall walkway trail along the river gorge, while an easygoing half-mile stroll on the viewpoint trail via the ornamental gardens also provides lovely views (£5 parking fee, daily 10:00-dusk, trail map available at café onsite, tel. 028/7034-0870, www.nidirect.gov.uk).

Getting There: The entry is off A-43 (via A-26; eight miles south of Cushendall, follow signs).

Nearby: Continue along the A-2 scenic coastal route and take a short jog up to Cushendall, where there's a nice beach for a picnic, or just head south on A-2 toward the Gobbins Cliff Path and the castle at Carrickfergus (see listings in the Belfast chapter).

BELFAST

Northern Ireland's capital city, Belfast is best known for its role in the Troubles, and as the birthplace of the *Titanic* (and many other ships that didn't sink).

Today the historic Titanic Quarter symbolizes the rise of Belfast. The city is bristling with cranes and busy with tourists. It's hard to believe that the bright and bustling pedestrian center was once a subdued, traffic-free security zone. These days, while Catholics and Protestants still generally live and study in segregated zones, they are totally integrated where they work—and they all root for the Belfast Giants ice hockey team. Aggressive sectarian murals are slowly being repainted with scenes celebrating heritage pride... less carnage, more culture. It feels like a new morning in Belfast.

PLANNING YOUR TIME

If you're staying in Dublin and not planning on visiting Belfast, reconsider. A long day trip from Dublin to Belfast is one of the most interesting days you could have anywhere in Ireland. It's just a two-hour train ride away—about €40 for "day return" tickets, and much less if bought online in advance.

Day Trip from Dublin

Here's how I'd do it (any day but Sun when trains don't run as early or late):

7:35	Catch the train from Dublin's Connolly Station
9:45	Arrive at Belfast's Lanyon Place/Central Station
11:00	Take the free City Hall tour, browse the pedestrian zone, have lunch

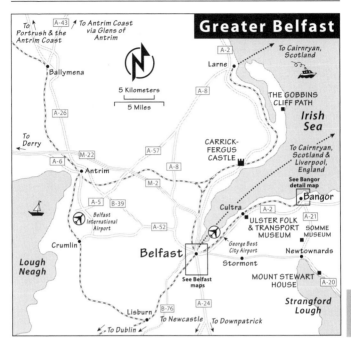

13:00 Take a taxi tour of the sectarian neighborhoods in West Belfast
15:00 Visit the Titanic Belfast Museum (after midday crowds subside)
17:00 Dinner in the Titanic Quarter or Cathedral Quarter
20:00 Catch the train back to Dublin

With More Time

If you're circling Ireland by car, Belfast can easily fill two days of sightseeing. On the first day, follow my day-trip itinerary. On the second day, consider side-tripping to sights outside of town, such as the Ulster Folk Park and Transport Museum or Carrickfergus Castle.

Orientation to Belfast

Belfast is flat and spread out. Restaurants and live music venues are all within walking distance of the town center. When planning, think of Belfast as having four sightseeing zones:

Central Belfast: The perfectly walkable city center has a dozen or so mostly minor sights that are never crowded and often free. Review the options and lace together your own plan (keeping opening days and times in mind). Sights include Donegall Square,

City Hall, pedestrian shopping areas, and the Cathedral Quarter with its lively night scene.

West Belfast: The working-class, sectarian neighborhoods along Falls Road and Shankill Road, while walkable, are much more interesting with a taxi tour (90 minutes, inexpensive, and almost as easy as hailing a taxi).

Titanic Quarter: The northeast bank of the River Lagan is dominated by the Titanic Belfast Museum, but there's much more here, including a wonderful riverside stroll with a string of sightseeing stops along the way.

South Belfast: This neighborhood is really just a strategic hit on the great Ulster Museum or Botanic Gardens, depending on your interest. This is where you'll find more cozy B&B guesthouses, rather than just chain hotels.

TOURIST INFORMATION

The modern TI (look for *Visit Belfast* sign) faces City Hall and has a courteous staff and baggage storage (£4/bag for 4 hours, £6/bag for 8 hours; Mon-Sat 9:00-17:30, June-Sept until 19:00, Sun 11:00-16:00 year-round; 9 Donegall Square North, tel. 028/9024-6609, http://visitbelfast.com). City walking tours depart from the TI (see "Tours in Belfast," later). Pick up a free copy of *Visit Belfast*, which lists all the sightseeing and evening entertainment options.

ARRIVAL IN BELFAST

By Train: Arriving at Belfast's Lanyon Place/Central Station, take the Centrelink bus, which loops to Donegall Square, where you'll find City Hall and the TI (4/hour, free with any train or bus ticket, the stop is out the station and 50 yards to the right). Allow £6 for a taxi to Donegall Square or the Titanic Belfast Museum; £10 to my accommodation listings south of the university.

Slower trains arc through the city, stopping at several downtown stations, including Great Victoria Street Station (most central, near Donegall Square and most hotels) and Botanic Station (close to the university, Botanic Gardens, and some recommended lodgings). It's easy and cheap to connect stations by train (£1.50).

If day-tripping into Belfast from Bangor, use the station closest to your targeted sights. Note that trains cost the same from Bangor to all three Belfast stations (Lanyon Place/Central, Great Victoria Street, and Botanic).

Belfast's Troubled History

Seventeenth-century Belfast was just a village. With the influx, or "plantation," of mostly Scottish settlers—and the subjugation of the native Irish—Belfast blossomed, spurred by the success of local industries. The city built many of the world's biggest and finest ships. And when the American Civil War shut down the US cotton industry, the linen mills of Belfast were beneficiaries. In fact Belfast became known as "Linen-opolis."

The Industrial Revolution took root in Belfast with a vengeance. While the rest of Ireland remained rural and agricultural, Belfast earned another nickname, "Old Smoke," during the time when many of the brick buildings that you'll see today were built.

The year 1888 marked the birth of modern Belfast. After Queen Victoria granted Belfast city status, it boomed. The population (only 20,000 in 1800) reached 350,000 by 1900. And its citizens built Belfast's centerpiece—its grand City Hall.

Belfast was also busy building ships, from transoceanic liners like the ill-fated *Titanic* to naval vessels during the world wars. (Belfast's famous shipyards were strategic enough to be the target of four German Luftwaffe bombing raids in World War II.) Two huge, mustard-colored, rectangular gantry cranes (built in the 1970s, and once the biggest in the world, nicknamed Samson and Goliath) stand like idle giants over the shipyards—a reminder of Belfast's shipbuilding might.

Of course, the sectarian Troubles ravaged Belfast along with the rest of Northern Ireland from 1969 to 1998—a time when downtown Belfast was ringed with security checks and nearly shut down at night. There was almost no tourism for two decades (and only a few pubs downtown). Thankfully, at the beginning of the 21st century, the peace process began to take root, and investments from south of the border—the Republic of Ireland—injected new life into the dejected shipyards where the *Titanic* was built.

Still, it's a fragile peace. Hateful bonfires, built a month before they're set ablaze, still scorch the pavement in working-class Protestant neighborhoods each July. Pubs with security gates are reminders that the island is still split—and 900,000 Protestant Unionists in the North prefer it that way.

BELFAST

By Car: Driving in Belfast is a pain. Avoid it if possible. Street parking in the city center is geared for short stops (use pay-and-display machines, £0.30/15 minutes, one-hour maximum, Mon-Sat 8:00-18:00, free in evenings and on Sun).

By Plane: For information on Belfast's airports, see the "Belfast Connections" section on page 102.

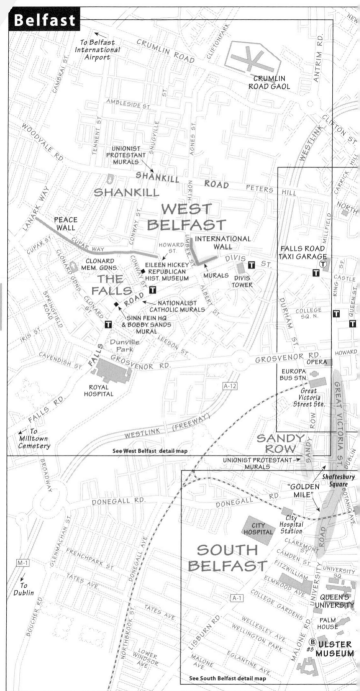

Belfast

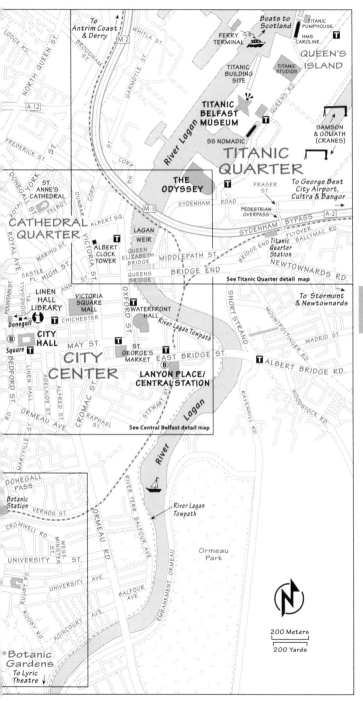

HELPFUL HINTS

Belfast Visitor Pass: This pass combines sightseeing discounts with iLink smartcards for free bus, rail, and tram rides within the Belfast Visitor Pass Zone (downtown Belfast as far out as the Ulster Folk Park and Transport Museum in Cultra, but not as far as Carrickfergus or Bangor). You'll save money with the one-day pass if you visit the Titanic Belfast Museum (£3 discount) and the Ulster Folk Park and Transport Museum (30 percent discount) and connect them by train or bus (free with pass). Buy it at the TI, any train station, either airport, Europa Bus station, or online (1-day pass-£6, 2 consecutive days-£11, 3 days-£14.50, tel. 028/9066-6630, www.translink.co.uk).

Place Names: Place names in Belfast can be confusing. The main train station, long called "Central Station," is now called "Lanyon Place" (many old maps have yet to get the memo). The key reference point in the center is Donegall Square, which is right in front of City Hall. The biggest attraction in town, the museum about the *Titanic,* is branded as "Titanic Belfast." For clarity in this chapter, I'll call it the "Titanic Belfast Museum."

Market: On Friday, Saturday, and Sunday, the Victorian confines of **St. George's Market** are a commotion of commerce and a people-watching delight (see page 75).

Shopping Mall: Victoria Square is a glitzy American-style mall where you can find whatever you need (3 blocks east of City Hall—bordered by Chichester, Victoria, Ann, and Montgomery streets; www.victoriasquare.com).

Phone Tips: For details on making calls between the Republic of Ireland and Northern Ireland, see page 110.

Laundry: Globe Launderers has both self-serve and drop-off service (Mon-Fri 8:00-21:00, Sat until 18:00, Sun 12:00-18:00, 37 Botanic Avenue, tel. 028/9024-3956). **Whistle Cleaners** is handy to hotels south of the university (drop-off service, Mon-Fri 8:30-18:00, Sat 9:00-17:30, closed Sun, 160 Lisburn Road, at intersection with Eglantine Avenue, tel. 028/9038-1297). For locations, see the map on page 91.

Bike Rental: Belfast City Bikes rents bikes of all types, from fancy electric (£50/day) down to Dorothy-and-Toto style (£10/day). It's located at Norm's Bikes, near the Cathedral Quarter (Unit 12 Smithfield Marketplace, Winetavern Street, mobile 079-8081-6057, www.belfastcitybiketours.com). They also offer bike tours (see "Tours in Belfast," later).

GETTING AROUND BELFAST

If you line up your sightseeing logically, you can do most of this flat city on foot. But for more far-flung sights, the train, bus, or tram can be useful. If you plan to use public transit, consider the Belfast Visitor Pass (see "Helpful Hints," earlier).

By Train, Bus, or Tram: Translink operates Belfast's system of trains, buses, and trams (tel. 028/9066-6630, www.translink.co.uk).

At any **train** station, ask about iLink smartcards, which cover one day of unlimited train, tram, and bus travel. The Zone 1 card (£6) covers the city center, Cultra (Ulster Folk Park and Transport Museum), and George Best Belfast City Airport. The handy Zone 2 card (£11) adds Bangor and Carrickfergus Castle. The Zone 3 card (£14.50) is only useful for reaching Belfast's distant international airport. Zone 4 (£17.50) gets you anywhere in Northern Ireland, including Portrush and Derry. For those lingering in the North, one-week cards offer even better deals. Without a pass, if you're traveling from Belfast to only one destination—Carrickfergus Castle, Cultra, or Bangor—a "day return" ticket is cheaper than two one-way tickets.

Pink-and-white city **buses** go from Donegall Square East to Malone Road and my recommended accommodations (any #8 bus, 3/hour, covered by iLink smartcards, otherwise £2.40, £4.20 all-day pass, cheaper after 9:30 and on Sun). Sunday service is less frequent.

The slick two-line Glider **tram** system opened in 2018 and connects East and West Belfast (line #G1) and downtown with the Titanic Quarter (line #G2). Rides on these "trams on wheels" cost £2 (6/hour, ticket machines at each stop, covered by iLink smartcards). The #G2 is particularly handy for travelers connecting City Hall with all the Titanic area sights.

By Taxi: Taxis are reasonable (£3 drop charge plus £1.60/ mile) and a good option—but they can be hard to flag down. Locals routinely call for a cab, as do restaurants and hotels for their guests. Try **Valu Cabs** (tel. 028/9080-9080). If you're going up Falls Road, ride a shared cab (explained later, under "Touring the Sectarian Neighborhoods"). Uber is nicknamed "Uber Expensive" here—it doesn't work well.

Tours in Belfast

Beyond the tours listed below, I highly recommend visiting the **sectarian neighborhoods** in West Belfast on a taxi or walking tour (see "Touring the Sectarian Neighborhoods" on page 76).

ON FOOT

Belfast's history is more interesting than its actual sights (and its people are really fun to get to know). A guided walk makes a lot of sense here. In fact, you could take several guided walks, as each one would be filled with entertaining insights on different angles of the city (and tours are relatively cheap).

BELFAST

Walking Tours

Free tours are actually "pay what you think it's worth" tours, led by locals who spin a good yarn while sharing the basics of the city. These tours take a couple hours and leave from in front of City Hall and the TI (daily in season at 11:00 and 14:30, just show up, www.belfastfreewalkingtour.com).

Experience Belfast Tours, a step up, introduces you to the city's 300-year history. Their "Hidden Belfast" tour includes City Hall, the Cathedral Quarter, and the Linen Hall Library (£10, 1 hour, daily at 11:00 and 13:00). Their "Troubles" tour covers everything on the "Hidden" tour plus the River Lagan and Belfast's political murals (£15, 2.5 hours, daily at 10:00). Both meet in front of the City Hall main gate facing Donegall Square North (mobile 077-7164-0746, https://experiencebelfast.com).

Belfast Hidden Tours focuses on the culture of North Belfast, going heavy on trade and industry with a sprinkling of rebel sedition and Luftwaffe destruction, while leading visitors to less obvious corners of the city (£10, 1 hour; March-Oct daily at 10:00, 12:00, and 14:00; meet at TI, mobile 079-7189-5746, www.belfasthiddentours.com).

Street Art Tours

Belfast is gaining notoriety for its colorful and edgy **street art.** Rather than sectarian political murals, this is pure urban art with a statement that is hard to understand without a local guide. Ask at the TI or search the web for companies offering these walks.

Food Tours

Taste & Tour offers a palate-pleasing array of food, beer, and whiskey tours, generally in small groups with six stops and lots of fun. Their basic food tour runs Friday and Saturday only and books up well in advance (£60, 3-4 hours, departure points vary, tel. 028/9045-7723, www.tasteandtour.co.uk).

Local Guides

Dee Morgan is smart and delightful. She grew up on Falls Road and can tailor your tour to history, food, politics, or music (£180/half-day, info@deetoursireland.com).

Susie Millar is a sharp former BBC TV reporter with family connections to the *Titanic* tragedy. She can also take you farther afield by car (yours or hers, 3-hour tour-£30/person, mobile 078-5271-6655, www.titanictours-belfast.co.uk).

Lynn Corken is another knowledgeable and flexible Jill-of-all-guiding trades, with a passion for her hometown, politics, history, and Van Morrison (on foot or with her car, £100/half-day, £200/day, mobile 077-7910-2448, lynncorken@hotmail.co.uk).

ON WHEELS
▲Hop-On, Hop-Off Bus Tours

City Sightseeing offers the best quick introduction to the city's political and social history. Their open-top, double-decker buses

link major sights and landmarks, including the Catholic and Protestant working-class neighborhoods, the Stormont Parliament building, Titanic Belfast Museum, and City Hall, with commentary on political murals and places of interest. The route has convenient stops near several recommended hotels: Fisherwick Place (Jurys Inn), Shaftsbury Square (Benedicts Hotel and Belfast International City Hostel), and Malone Road (Malone Lodge and Wellington Park Hotel). Pay cash on the bus (£12.50/24 hours, £14/48 hours, 2/hour, fewer in winter, daily 10:00-16:00, 20 stops, 1.5-hour loop; departs from Castle Place on High Street, 2 blocks west of Albert Memorial Clock Tower; tel. 028/9032-1321, http://belfastcitysightseeing.com).

City Tours offers a route with more than 20 stops. It starts on High Street (near Albert Clock), then veers westward to take in Falls and Shankill roads (£11/24 hours, £12.50/72 hours, pay cash on bus or book in advance, 2/hour, daily 9:45-16:45, tel. 028/9032-1912, www.citytoursbelfast.com).

Countryside Bus Tours

McComb's offers several big-bus tours, day-tripping out of Belfast to distant points. Their "Giant's Causeway Tour" visits Carrickfergus Castle (photo stop), the Giant's Causeway, Dunluce Castle (photo stop), and Carrick-a-Rede Rope Bridge (£25, daily depending on demand, book through and depart from recommended Belfast International City Hostel, pickup around 9:00, back to Belfast by 19:00). Their *"Game of Thrones* Tour" visits many of the sites where the hit TV series was filmed (£35, pickup at 8:30, return by 19:00, tel. 028/9031-5333, www.mccombscoaches.com).

Bike Tours

Belfast City Bikes offers two tours—one in the city and one in the countryside. The "City Bike Tour" stays urban for nine miles and rides thorough the Titanic Quarter, St. Georges Market, and Queen's University (£30, 3 hours). The "Bike and Brew Tour" goes into the countryside for 12 miles along the River Lagan Towpath, ending at the Hilden Brewery (£50 plus £4 train trip back to Belfast, lunch included, 4 hours). Both depart Thu-Sun at 10:00 (helmets included, reserve ahead—for contact info see "Bike Rental" under "Helpful Hints," earlier).

BY BOAT
Harbor Tours

The **Lagan Boat Company** offers a one-hour tour with an entertaining guide showing the shipyards, the fruits of the city's £800 million investment in its harbor, and the rusty *Titanic* heritage (£12; April-Oct daily sailings at 12:30, 14:00, and 15:30; fewer off-season, tel. 028/9024-0124, www.laganboatcompany.com, Joyce). Tours depart from near the Lagan Weir just past the Albert Clock Tower.

Sights in Belfast

Belfast breaks down into four sightseeing zones: Central Belfast (government center, shopping and restaurant district, trendy nightlife), West Belfast (both Republican and Loyalist sectarian neighborhoods), the Titanic Quarter (superstar museum and riverside walk), and South Belfast (college vibe, good hotels and B&Bs, gardens and history museum).

CENTRAL BELFAST

The sights of central Belfast are mostly minor but fun to check out. Nearly all are within a ten-minute walk of City Hall.

Donegall Square and Nearby
▲▲City Hall

This grand structure's 173-foot-tall copper dome dominates Donegall Square at the center of town. Built between 1898 and 1906, with its statue of Queen Victoria scowling down Belfast's main drag and the Neoclassical dome looming behind her, City Hall is a stirring sight. Free tours of the building run daily, and the worthwhile 16-room Belfast History and Culture exhibit fills the ground floor. It covers the history of the city, culture, industry, the World War II bombings, and the Troubles.

Cost and Hours: City Hall—free, daily 8:00-17:00; Belfast History and Culture exhibit—free, daily 9:00-17:00; audioguide-£3.50; Bobbin coffee shop on ground floor, tel. 028/9032-0202, www.belfastcity.gov.uk/cityhall.

Tours: Free 45-minute tours run Mon-Fri at 10:00, 11:00, 14:00, 15:00, and 16:00; Sat-Sun at 12:00, 14:00, 15:00, and 16:00 (fewer off-season); drop by, call, or check online to confirm schedule and book a spot.

Linen Hall Library
Across the street from City Hall, the 200-year-old Linen Hall Library welcomes guests (notice the red hand above the front door facing Donegall Square North; for more on its meaning, see the sidebar on page 92). Described as "Ulster's attic," the library takes pride in being a neutral space where anyone trying to make sense of the sectarian conflict can view the "Troubled Images," a historical collection of engrossing political posters. The library has a fine hardbound ambience and a royal newspaper reading room. Climb to the top floor and then go down the back staircase, where the walls are lined with fascinating original posters from those tough times.

Cost and Hours: Free, Mon-Fri 9:30-17:30, closed Sat-Sun, 45-minute tours (£5) run daily at 10:30, 17 Donegall Square North, tel. 028/9032-1707, www.linenhall.com.

Donegall Square to the Cathedral Quarter
This little stroll through Belfast's shopping district takes you from City Hall to the Cathedral Quarter in 10 minutes or less.

Donegall Square: The front yard of City Hall is littered with statues of historic figures. Take a close look at the **Queen Victoria** monument. It celebrates the industrial might of Belfast: shipping, linen (the woman with the bobbin), and education (the student). At her right is a reminder of how Belfast was a springboard for the European battlefront in World War II—a **monument** dedicated by General Dwight D. Eisenhower in 1945 to the more than 100,000 US troops who were stationed in Northern Ireland. And around to the left (as you face the building), you'll find the thought-provoking **Titanic Memorial Garden.**

Donegall Place: City Hall faces the commercial heart of Belfast. With your back to City Hall, follow Queen Victoria's gaze across the square and down the shopping street called Donegall Place (note the **TI** on the left). Victoria would recognize the fine 19th-century brick buildings—built in the Scottish Baronial style when the Scots dominated Belfast. But she'd be amazed by the changes since then. As a key shipbuilding and industrial port, Belfast was bombed by the Germans in World War II. (On the worst night of bombing more than 900 died.) And, with the Troubles killing the economy in the last decades of the 20th century, little

Belfast at a Glance

▲▲▲**Titanic Belfast Museum** Excellent high-tech exhibit covering the famously infamous ship and local shipbuilding, in a stunning structure on the site where the *Titanic* was built. **Hours:** Daily June-Aug 8:30-19:00, April-May and Sept 9:00-18:00; Oct-March 10:00-17:00. See page 88.

▲▲▲**Sectarian Neighborhoods Taxi Tours** Local cabbies drive visitors through West Belfast's Falls Road and Shankill Road neighborhoods, offering personal perspectives on the slowly fading Troubles. See page 76.

▲▲**City Hall** Central Belfast's polished and majestic celebration of Victorian-era pride built with industrial wealth. **Hours:** Daily 8:00-17:00. See page 66.

▲▲**Live Music** For the cost of a beer, connect with Belfast's culture, people, and music in a pub. **Hours:** Nightly after 21:30. See page 96.

▲**HMS *Caroline*** WWI battleship that looks just like it did at the Battle of Jutland in 1916. **Hours:** Daily 10:00-17:00. See page 89.

▲**St. George's Market** Thriving scene filling a huge Victorian market hall with artisans, junk dealers, street food, and fun. **Hours:** Fri-Sun 9:00-15:00. See page 75.

▲**Ulster Museum** Mixed bag of local artifacts, natural history, and coverage of political events; a good rainy-day option near Queen's University. **Hours:** Tue-Sun 10:00-17:00, closed Mon. See page 90.

BELFAST

was built. With peace in 1998—and government investing to subsidize that peace—the 21st century has been one big building boom.

Ahead of you, look for a **stained-glass window.** While the *Titanic* connection is still strong, the latest craze here is *Game of Thrones* tourism (much of the show was filmed in Northern Ireland). To recognize the show's importance to Ireland's film industry, and please countless fans, Belfast erected six stained-glass windows around town (one for each episode of the final season).

Walk down Donegal Place

▲**Botanic Gardens** Belfast's best green space, featuring the Palm House loaded with delicate tropical vegetation. **Hours:** Gardens daily 7:30 until dusk; Palm House daily 10:00-17:00, Oct-March until 16:00. See page 91.

Near Belfast
▲▲**Ulster Folk Park and Transport Museum** A glimpse into Northern Ireland's hardworking heritage, split between a charming re-creation of past rural life and halls of vehicular innovation (8 miles east of Belfast). **Hours:** March-Sept Tue-Sun 10:00-17:00; Oct-Feb Tue-Fri 10:00-16:00, Sat-Sun from 11:00; closed Mon year-round. See page 93.

▲**Carrickfergus Castle** Northern Ireland's first and most important fortified refuge for invading 12th-century Normans (14 miles northeast of Belfast). **Hours:** Daily 9:00-17:00, Oct-March until 16:00. See page 94.

▲**The Gobbins** Rugged, unique, wave-splashed hiking trail cut into coastal rock, accessible by guided tour (34 miles northeast of Belfast). **Hours:** Visitors center daily 9:30-17:30, guided hikes about hourly in good weather. See page 94.

Near Bangor
▲**Mount Stewart House** Fine 18th-century manor house displaying ruling-class affluence, surrounded by lush and calming gardens (18 miles east of Belfast). **Hours:** Daily 11:00-17:00, closed Nov-Feb. See page 106.

BELFAST

past the **eight stylized sails** celebrating the great ships built here for the White Star Line (their names all end in "ic").

Shopping Streets: At the sail for the *Celtic*, cruise to the right down Castle Lane. This is the busker zone, alive with street music on nice days. Ahead is the striking, modern **"Spirit of Belfast" statue** (a.k.a. the "Onion Rings"). That "spirit" is the spirit of industry—specifically linen and shipbuilding (light and strong, like the statue). The spirit could also be the resilience of this city with its complicated history and the oversized impact it's had in a broader sense (for example, at least 17 US presidents have some Ulster roots).

To the right of the statue (down William Street) is the sleek and modern **Victoria Square Shopping Center,** worth a visit for its free elevator to the top of its glass dome offering grand city

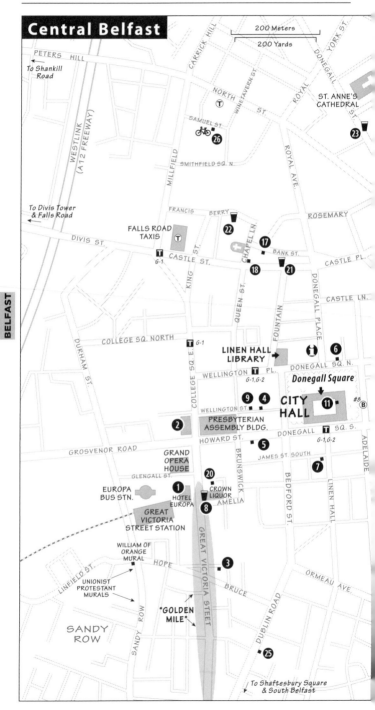

Central Belfast

BELFAST

200 Meters
200 Yards

PETERS HILL

To Shankill
Road

WESTLINK (A12 FREEWAY)

NORTH ST.

WHETAVERN ST.

CARRICK HILL

YORK ST.

DONEGALL

ROYAL ST.

ST. ANNE'S
CATHEDRAL

23

SAMUEL ST.

26

MILLFIELD

SMITHFIELD SQ. N.

ROYAL AVE.

ROSEMARY

FRANCIS

BERRY

22

CHAPEL LN.

17

BANK ST.

21

CASTLE PL.

To Divis Tower
& Falls Road

DIVIS ST.

FALLS ROAD
TAXIS

CASTLE ST.

G-1

KING ST.

QUEEN ST.

18

FOUNTAIN

DONEGALL PLACE

CASTLE LN.

COLLEGE SQ. NORTH

G-1

DURHAM ST.

COLLEGE SQ. E.

LINEN HALL
LIBRARY

6

DONEGALL SQ. N.

WELLINGTON PL.

G-1, G-2

Donegall Square

2

WELLINGTON ST.

9 4

CITY
HALL

11

#8

B

GROSVENOR ROAD

PRESBYTERIAN
ASSEMBLY BLDG.

HOWARD ST.

DONEGALL SQ. S.

G-1, G-2

ADELAIDE

GRAND
OPERA
HOUSE

5

BRUNSWICK

JAMES ST. SOUTH

7

GLENGALL ST.

EUROPA BUS STN.

1

HOTEL
EUROPA

20

CROWN
LIQUOR

8

AMELIA

BEDFORD ST.

LINEN HALL

GREAT
VICTORIA
STREET STATION

WILLIAM OF
ORANGE MURAL

HOPE

3

GREAT VICTORIA STREET

UNIONIST
PROTESTANT
MURALS

LINFIELD ST.

SANDY ROW

BRUCE

DUBLIN ROAD

ORMEAU AVE.

"GOLDEN
MILE"

SANDY
ROW

25

To Shaftesbury Square
& South Belfast

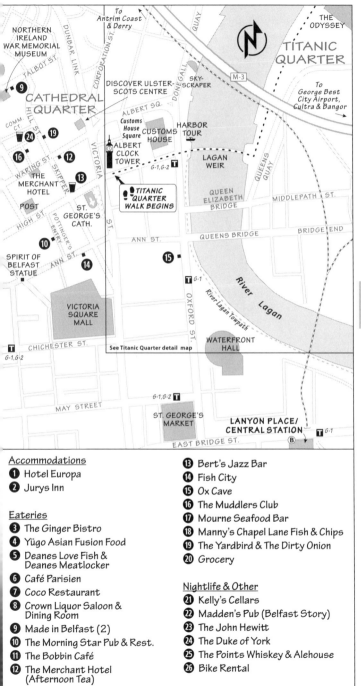

Accommodations
1 Hotel Europa
2 Jurys Inn

Eateries
3 The Ginger Bistro
4 Yūgo Asian Fusion Food
5 Deanes Love Fish & Deanes Meatlocker
6 Café Parisien
7 Coco Restaurant
8 Crown Liquor Saloon & Dining Room
9 Made in Belfast (2)
10 The Morning Star Pub & Rest.
11 The Bobbin Café
12 The Merchant Hotel (Afternoon Tea)
13 Bert's Jazz Bar
14 Fish City
15 Ox Cave
16 The Muddlers Club
17 Mourne Seafood Bar
18 Manny's Chapel Lane Fish & Chips
19 The Yardbird & The Dirty Onion
20 Grocery

Nightlife & Other
21 Kelly's Cellars
22 Madden's Pub (Belfast Story)
23 The John Hewitt
24 The Duke of York
25 The Points Whiskey & Alehouse
26 Bike Rental

views. The center has lots of movies, restaurants, and shops (Mon-Sat 9:30-18:00, Wed-Fri until 21:00, Sun 13:00-18:00).

Victoria Street: Exiting the mall, it's a short walk up Victoria Street to the Albert Memorial Clock Tower (and the start of my "Titanic Quarter Walk") and the Cathedral Quarter, described later in this section.

The Golden Mile

The "Golden Mile" is the overstated nickname of a Belfast entertainment zone with a few interesting sights on Great Victoria Street, just southwest of City Hall.

The **Presbyterian Assembly Building,** a fine example of Scottish Baronial architecture, has a welcoming little visitor exhibition that tells the story of the Presbyterians in Northern Ireland. They were discriminated against (like the Roman Catholics) because they also refused to embrace the High Church approach to Christianity as dictated by the Anglican Church. You'll learn about the founder, John Knox, and find out why a pitch pipe, which made singing hymns without accompaniment possible, was necessary (free, Mon-Fri 9:30-17:00, closed Sat-Sun, across from Jury's Inn at 2 Fisherwick Place).

The **Grand Opera House,** originally built in 1895, bombed and rebuilt in 1991, and bombed and rebuilt again in 1993, is extravagantly Victorian and *the* place to take in a concert, play, or opera (ticket office open Mon-Sat 10:00-17:00, closed Sun; ticket office to right of main front door on Great Victoria Street, tel. 028/9024-1919, www.goh.co.uk). The nearby **Hotel Europa,** considered to be the most-bombed hotel in the world (33 times during the Troubles), actually feels pretty laid-back today.

The Crown Liquor Saloon is the ultimate gin palace. Built in 1849 (when Catholic Ireland was suffering through the Great Potato Famine), its mahogany, glass, and marble interior is a trip back into the days of Queen Victoria. Wander through and imagine the snugs (booths designed to provide a little privacy for un-Victorian behavior) before the invasion of selfie-snapping tourists. Upstairs, the recommended Crown Dining Room serves pub grub and is decorated with historic photos.

Cathedral Quarter

Tucked between St. Anne's Cathedral and the River Lagan, this rejuvenating district is busy with shoppers by day and clubbers by night. And, being the oldest part of Belfast, it's full of history. Be-

fore World War I, this was the whiskey warehouse district—at a time when the Belfast region produced about half of all Irish whiskey.

While today's Cathedral District has a few minor sights, the big attraction is its night-life—restaurants, clubs, and pubs. For the epicenter of this zone, head for the intersection of **Hill Street and Commercial Court** and peek into nearby breezeways. As you explore, you'll find a maze of narrow streets, pubs named for the colorful characters that gave the city its many legends, and creative street-art murals that hint at the artistic spirit and still-feisty edginess of Belfast.

The Cathedral Quarter extends to the old merchant district, with its Victorian-era **Customs House** backed up to the river.

Nearby, at the intersection of High Street and Victoria Street, is Belfast's "Little Big Ben," the **Albert Memorial Clock Tower.** The tower was built in 1870 to honor to Queen Victoria's beloved Prince Albert, nine years after he died. It sits on the birthplace of the city, where Belfast was founded over a thousand years ago on a little river that later became High Street. (The little river still runs under the street.) The tower famously leans (as it was built on an unstable riverbank), and locals say Albert looks like he's ready to leap to safety when the tower finally falls.

About 50 yards in front of Albert is **St. George's Church** (with an interesting history posted at its gate). A church has stood here for over a millenium.

The clock tower is the start of my "Titanic Quarter Walk" (see page 83).

St. Anne's Cathedral
Also known as Belfast Cathedral, this Anglican church was built in the early 1900s, at the peak of Belfast's industrial power. Its mosaics and stained glass are colorful and modern. Lord Edward Carson, the fervent Unionist attorney who put Oscar Wilde behind bars—and whose Machiavellian political maneuverings ensured the creation of Northern Ireland in 1921—is buried here. The structure was nearly destroyed by a Luftwaffe bomb in 1941.

1916

This pivotal year means vastly different things to Northern Ireland's two communities. When you say "1776" to most Americans, it means revolution and independence from tyranny. But when you say "1916" to someone in Northern Ireland, the response depends on who's talking.

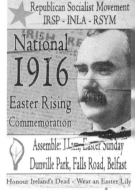

To Nationalists (who are usually Catholic), "1916" brings to mind the Easter Rising—which took place in Dublin in April of that year and was the beginning of the end of 750 years of British rule for most of Ireland. Some Nationalist murals still use images of Dublin's rebel headquarters or martyred leaders like Patrick Pearse and James Connolly. To this community, 1916 emphasizes their proud Gaelic identity, their willingness to fight to preserve it, and their stubborn anti-British attitude.

To Unionists (who are usually Protestant), "1916" means the brutal WWI Battle of the Somme in France, which began that July. (For more on the Somme, visit the Somme Museum in Bangor.) Although both Catholic and Protestant soldiers died in this long and costly battle, the first wave of young men who went over the top were the sons of proud Ulster Unionists. The Unionists hoped this blood sacrifice would prove their loyalty to the Crown—and assure that the British would never let them be gobbled up by an Irish Nationalist state (a possible scenario just before the Great War's outbreak). You'll see Tommies heroically climbing out of their trenches in some of Belfast's Unionist murals. For the Unionists, 1916 is synonymous with devout, almost righteously divine, Britishness.

Today, the sleek "Spire of Hope" (added in 2007) is a 130-foot-tall witness to God's love of Belfast—in the form of a spike like the Spire in Dublin—but much shorter. Goofy nicknames are an Irish passion: This one's dubbed "The Rod to God."

Cost and Hours: £5, Mon-Sat 9:00-17:00, evensong Mon-Fri at 17:30 (Sept-June) and Sun at 15:30, Donegall Street, tel. 028/9032-8332.

Northern Ireland War Memorial

Across the street from St. Anne's, this one-room sanctuary is dedicated to the lives lived and lost in this corner of the UK during World War II. Coverage includes the American troops based here during the war and the damage done by multiple German bombing raids during the Blitz.

Cost and Hours: Free, Mon-Fri 10:00-16:30, closed Sat-Sun, 21 Talbot Street, tel. 028/9032-0392, www.niwarmemorial.org.

Discover Ulster-Scots Centre

This bright and inviting gallery is designed to promote the Ulster-Scots heritage. Ulster and Scotland are 13 miles apart, and this exhibit feels almost like propaganda, asserting that prehistoric Scots migrated from northeastern Ireland—thus, the cultures are rightfully intertwined. If your heritage is Scots-Irish (as they became known in America) this drills home the impact Ulstermen and women had in building America and is a good place to begin your genealogy research.

Cost and Hours: Free, Mon-Fri 10:00-16:00, closed Sat-Sun, one block from clock tower at 1 Victoria Street, tel. 028/9043-6710, http://discoverulsterscots.com.

The Merchant Hotel

One of the finest buildings in town (34 Waring Street), this was once the headquarters of the Ulster Bank. Back when this was built

(mid-1800s) most people didn't have access to real banking, so banks were designed with over-the-top extravagance to give their aristocratic clientele confidence. In modern times, banking has changed, and all over Britain such dazzling mansions of finance have been vacated and often turned into fancy restaurants. Its recommended Bert's Jazz Bar is famous for its cocktails and in the Great Room, under a grand dome and the largest chandelier in Ireland, people dress up for the ritual of afternoon tea (see "Eating in Belfast," later). You're welcome to poke around.

East of Donegall Square
▲St. George's Market

This was once the largest covered produce market in Ireland. Today the farmers are gone and everyone else, it seems, has moved in. Three days a week (Fri-Sun, about 9:00-15:00) St. George's Market becomes a thriving arts, crafts, and flea market with a few fish and produce stalls to round things out. With a diverse array of street food and homemade goodies added to the mix, it's a fun place for lunch (five blocks east of City Hall, at the corner of Oxford and East Bridge streets, tel. 028/9043-5704).

SECTARIAN NEIGHBORHOODS IN WEST BELFAST

This slowly rejuvenating section of gritty West Belfast is home to two sectarian communities, living along the main roads to either side the Peace Wall: Unionist/Loyalists/Protestants along Shankill Road and Republicans/Nationalists/Catholics along Falls Road.

There's plenty to see in the sectarian hoods—especially murals. While you could simply (and safely) walk through these districts on your own, you'd be missing an easy opportunity to employ working-class locals who'd love to give you their firsthand, personal take on the Troubles from the perspective of their communities.

Here I list my recommendations for touring the sectarian neighborhoods, then describe the sights you'll see along the way. Before you go, make sure to read the "Understanding Belfast's Sectarian Neighborhoods" sidebar to give context to your visit.

Touring the Sectarian Neighborhoods

You can visit with a shared taxi, a private taxi tour, or on foot (with a guide, or your own—using cabs as you go). Hop-on, hop-off bus tours also drive these roads, but are impersonal and keep you at a distance. Skip them in favor of one of these options.

▲▲▲Sectarian Neighborhood Taxi Tours

Taxi tours are easy, inexpensive, and, for me, the most interesting 90 minutes you can have in Belfast. Quiz the cabbie (who grew up here) and pull over for photos. You'll get honest (if biased) viewpoints on the Troubles and local culture, see the political murals, and visit the many Troubles-related sights.

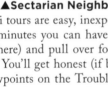

Falls Road Shared Taxi Service: The **West Belfast Taxi Association** (WBTA), run by a group of local Falls Road men, is located in the Castle Junction Car Park at the intersection of Castle and King streets. On the ground floor of this nine-story parking garage, a passenger terminal (entrance on King Street) connects travelers with old black cabs—and the only Irish-language signs in downtown Belfast.

These shared black cabs efficiently shuttle residents from out-

Understanding Belfast's Sectarian Neighborhoods

For centuries, Ireland has lived with tensions between Loyalists (also called Unionists, generally Protestants, who want to remain part of the United Kingdom, ruled from London) and Republicans (also called Nationalists, generally Roman Catholics, who want to be part of a united Ireland, independent from Great Britain). The Catholic Irish are the indigenous Irish and the Protestant loyalists are later arrivals, mostly "Scotch Irish," planted by London from Scotland in the north of Ireland.

A flare-up of violence in 1969 between these two communities led to a spontaneous mass reshuffling of working-class people in Belfast. Those who were minorities decided it was too dangerous to stay in the "wrong" sectarian neighborhood and moved into districts where they would be among their "tribe." Protestants left the Falls Road area for the Shankill Road area and Catholics left the Shankill Road area for the Falls Road area.

It's said that in these neighborhoods, the Catholics became more Irish than the Irish and the Protestants became more British than the British. Fighting between the two districts led the British army to build a "Peace Wall" to keep them apart. Paramilitary organizations on each side incited violence, and what came to be known as the Troubles began.

With two newly created ghettos dug in, it was a sad and bloody time that lasted until the Good Friday peace agreement in 1998. Since then, the bombings, assassinations, and burnings have stopped and peace has had the upper hand.

But Belfast is still segregated. Most working-class Protestants live and go to school with only Protestants. And the same is true in the Catholic community. The two groups have no trouble working or even socializing together downtown, but at night they retreat back to their separate enclaves.

The Peace Wall no longer stops projectiles and its gates are mostly open. There is peace. But there is no forgiveness: Murderers still cross paths with their victims' loved ones. Locals say it'll take another generation to be truly over the Troubles.

lying neighborhoods up and down Falls Road and to the city center. All shared cabs go up Falls Road, past Sinn Féin headquarters and lots of murals, to the Milltown Cemetery (sit in front and talk to the cabbie). Shared taxi cars have their roof sign removed and no meters. You'll pay £2/ride. You can get a cab at the Castle Junction Car Park, or anywhere along Falls Road, where easy-to-flag-down cabs run every minute or so in each direction. Just flag one down to stop it, and rap on the window to exit. Hop in and out.

This service originated almost 50 years ago at the beginning

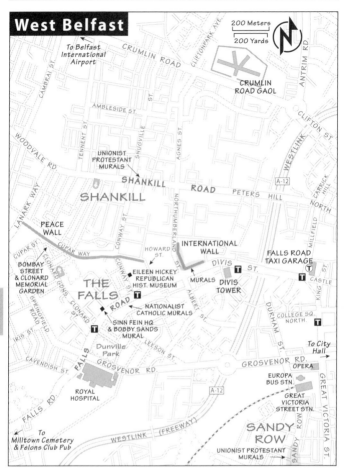

West Belfast

To Belfast
International
Airport

CRUMLIN ROAD

200 Meters
200 Yards

N

CRUMLIN
ROAD GAOL

AMBLESIDE ST.

UNIONIST
PROTESTANT
MURALS

SHANKILL

SHANKILL ROAD PETERS HILL

A-12

PEACE
WALL

INTERNATIONAL
WALL

FALLS ROAD
TAXI GARAGE

BOMBAY
STREET
& CLONARD
MEMORIAL
GARDEN

THE
FALLS

EILEEN HICKEY
REPUBLICAN
HIST. MUSEUM

DIVIS
MURALS DIVIS
TOWER

HOWARD
ST.

NATIONALIST
CATHOLIC MURALS

SINN FEIN HQ
& BOBBY SANDS
MURAL

Dunville
Park

GROSVENOR RD.

COLLEGE SQ.
NORTH.

To City
Hall

GROSVENOR RD.
OPERA

ROYAL
HOSPITAL

EUROPA
BUS STN.

A-12

GREAT
VICTORIA
STREET STN.

To
Milltown Cemetery
& Felons Club Pub

WESTLINK (FREEWAY)

SANDY
ROW

UNIONIST PROTESTANT
MURALS

BELFAST

of the Troubles, when locals would hijack city buses and use them as barricades in the street fighting. Because of this, city bus service was discontinued, and local sectarian groups established a shared taxi service. Although the buses are now running again, these cab rides are still a great value for their drivers' commentaries. You can also hire a cab for a private 90-minute tour (see next).

Black Taxi Tours of Falls Road: Nearly any of the WBTA cabs described above are ready and able to give private tours (£45 for 3 people, more for up to 6, 90 minutes). While the drivers are Republican, these days they venture into the Loyalist zone as well. Taxi tours work great in the rain, as the cabbie just parks and talks while you look out the window. Three is comfortable in a cab. More than that and you'll have a hard time seeing. Just drop into the WBTA Passenger Terminal and they'll set you up (Taxi Trax

Black Taxi Tours, tel. 028/9031-5777, mobile 078-9271-6660, www.taxitrax.com).

Cab Tours Belfast: This group of driver/guides from both communities (Catholic and Protestant) has teamed up and is committed to giving unbiased  dual-narrative tours. Their "Belfast Murals Tour" covers both neighborhoods and is a fascinating 90 minutes. As their £35 price covers two people and includes free pick up and drop-off within central Belfast, this can work very efficiently with your sightseeing day (mobile 077-1364-0647, www.cabtoursbelfast.com).

Sectarian Neighborhood Walking Tours

On your own, get a map and lace together the sights along Falls Road by walking the street. Walking mixes well with hopping into shared taxis (described earlier) that go up and down constantly. They are generally big black cabs without a *Taxi* sign on top and without meters. Wave and they'll stop. Rap the window and they'll let you out. Riding in one of these cabs, you'll certainly get to talk with local people.

Or consider one of the following **walking-tour companies.**

Coiste Irish Political Tours offers the Republican/Catholic community perspective on an extended, two-hour "Falls Road Murals" walking tour. Led by former IRA prisoners, you'll visit murals, gardens of remembrance, and peace walls, and get to know the community. Tours meet beside the Divis Tower (the solitary, purple 20-story apartment building at the east end of Divis Road) and end at Milltown Cemetery. Afterwards, you're invited for a complimentary glass of Guinness at the Felons Club Pub—run by former IRA prisoners (£10; Tue, Thu, and Sat at 10:00; Sun at 14:00; best to book in advance, tel. 028/9020-0770, www.coiste. ie).

Belfast Political Tours runs a unique tour called "Conflicting Stories" in which former combatants from each side show and tell their story: a Republican for Falls Road sights and then a Unionist for Shankill Road sights (£18, 3 hours, most days at 9:30 and 14:30, departs from Divis Tower, mobile 073-9358-5531, www. belfastpoliticaltour.com).

Sandy Row Walking Tours provides the Unionist/Loyalist point of view during 90-minute walks centering on Sandy Row, Belfast's oldest residential neighborhood. Tours go beyond the

Troubles to cover the city's industrial heritage, the Orange Order, both world wars, and historic local churches. They depart from the William of Orange mural at the intersection of Sandy Row and Linfield Road (£7.50; most days at 10:00, 12:00, and 14:00; call to book, mobile 079-0925-4849, www.historicsandyrow.co.uk).

Sights in the Sectarian Neighborhoods

The sectarian neighborhoods are known for their murals. People here are working class and most live in row houses. The end of a row house is ready made for a big political mural—and there are lots of them.

It's a land where one community's freedom fighter is another community's terrorist. Although fighters didn't actually wear military uniforms, they're often portrayed in uniform in proud murals. (On Shankill Road there are still murals that celebrate "Top Gun" patriots who killed lots of Roman Catholics.)

But with more peaceful times, the character of these murals is slowly changing. The government is helping fund programs that replace aggressive murals with positive ones. Paramilitary themes are gradually being covered over with images of pride in each neighborhood's culture. The *Titanic* was built primarily by proud Protestant Ulster stock and is often seen in their neighborhood murals—reflecting their industrious work ethic. And in the Catholic neighborhoods, you'll see more murals depicting mythological heroes from the days before the English came.

Shankill Road

In the Loyalist Shankill Road area there are plenty of vivid murals and lots of red, white, and blue. You'll see fields where bonfires are built, with piles of wood awaiting the next Orange Day, July 12—when Protestants march and burn huge fires (and when Catholics choose to leave town on vacation). There is a particularly interesting series of murals at Lower Shankill Estate. And at the edge of the area is the Crumlin Road Gaol, a prison where combatants (mostly Republicans) did time (described next).

Crumlin Road Gaol

This Victorian-era jail a half-mile to the north of Shankill Road was kept busy from 1846 to 1996 incarcerating people—men, women, and even children. Its purpose: to control the angry indigenous Irish. One-hour guided tours show how the prison was run, who was held here, and what was life like for the prisoners. You'll trace the jail's history from opening to closing, climb the tunnel to the derelict courthouse across the street, and visit actual cells where inmates lived (£12, open daily 10:00-16:30, tours at least hourly, book and confirm tours by phone, 53 Crumlin Road, tel. 028/9074-1500, www.crumlinroadgaol.com).

Peace Wall

The sad, corrugated structure called the Peace Wall runs a block or so north of Falls Road (along Cupar Way) separating the Catho-

lics from the Protestants in the Shankill Road area. The wall has five gates that open each day from about 8:00 to 18:00. On the Protestant side there is a long stretch where tour groups stop to write peaceful and hopeful messages.

The first cement wall was 20 feet high—it was later extended another 10 feet by a solid metal addition, and then another 15 feet with a metal screen. Seemingly high enough now to deter a projectile being lobbed over, this is one of many such walls erected in Belfast during the Troubles. Meant to be temporary, these barriers stay up because of old fears among the communities on both sides.

International Wall

Just past the gate on Townsend Street on the Republican side stretches the colorful, so-called "International Wall"—an L-shaped, two-block-long series of political murals that shows solidarity with other oppressed groups. (For example, Catholics in Ulster have a natural affinity with Basques in Spain and Palestinians in Israel). Along the Falls Road section of the International Wall are "current events" murals as up-to-date as last month.

Falls Road and Nearby

In the Catholic Falls Road area, you'll notice that the road signs are in two languages (Irish first). Sights include the many political murals, neighborhood memorial gardens, and Bombay Street, which the Protestants burned in 1969, igniting the Troubles. Next to the well-fortified Sinn Féin Press Office is a political gift-and-book shop. The powerful local Republican museum is two blocks away. Farther down Falls Road is the Milltown Cemetery where the hunger strikers are buried and revered as martyrs (all described next).

Sinn Féin Press Office: Near the bottom of Falls Road, at #51, is the press center for the hardline Republican party, Sinn Féin. While the press office is not open to the public, the adjacent **book-**

Bobby Sands MP
POET, GAEILGEOIR, REVOLUTIONARY, IRA VOLUNTEER.

EVERYONE REPUBLICAN OR OTHERWISE HAS THEIR OWN PARTICULAR ROLE TO PLAY

OUR REVENGE WILL BE THE LAUGHTER OF OUR CHILDREN

BELFAST

store (with an intriguing gift shop) is welcoming and worth a look. Page through books featuring color photos of the political murals that decorated these buildings. Money raised here supports the families of deceased IRA members. Around the corner is a big and bright mural remembering **Bobby Sands,** a member of parliament who led a hunger strike in prison with fellow inmates and starved himself to death to very effectively raise awareness of the Republican concerns.

Eileen Hickey Republican History Museum: This volunteer-run museum, tucked away in a residential complex, has a clear mission: "For Republican history to be told by Republicans. To educate our youth so they may understand why Republicans fought, died, and spent many years in prison for their beliefs." This is an unforgettable museum, with real (if totally biased) history shown and told by people who played a part in it (free, Tue-Sat 10:00-14:00, closed Sun-Mon, two blocks from Sinn Féin Press Office at 5 Conway Place, tel. 028/9024-0504, www. eileenhickeymuseum.com).

Bombay Street and Clonard Memorial Garden: About a 10-minute walk from the Sinn Féin Press Office is Bombay Street and the Clonard Memorial Garden. On August 15, 1969, Loyalists set fire to the Catholic homes and a monastery on this street. In the violence, a Republican teenager was killed. The burning of this Catholic street led to the "sorting out" of the communities and the building of the Peace Wall. Today you'll see Bombay Street nicely rebuilt, photos of the terrible event, and a peaceful memorial garden against the wall.

Milltown Cemetery: To reach the cemetery, take a taxi or the #G1 Glider tram to the Falls Park stop; it's too far to walk (cemetery open daily 9:00-16:00, 546 Falls Road, tel. 028/9061-3972). This burial site for Republican martyrs can be a pilgrimage for some. You'll walk past all the Gaelic crosses down to the far right-hand corner (closest to the highway), where little green railings set apart the IRA Roll of Honor from the thousands of other graves. These martyrs are treated like fallen soldiers. Notice the memorial to Bobby Sands and nine other hunger strikers. They starved themselves to death in the nearby Maze Prison in 1981, protesting for political prisoner status as opposed to terrorist criminal treatment (the prison closed in the fall of 2000).

Sandy Row

To the southwest of City Hall, Sandy Row is a smaller Unionist, Protestant working-class street just behind Hotel Europa that offers a cheap and easy way to get a dose of a sectarian neighborhood. From Hotel Europa, walk a block down Glengall Street, then turn left and walk for 10 minutes. A stop in a Unionist memorabilia shop, a pub, or one of the many cheap eateries here may give you an opportunity to talk to a local. Along the way you'll see murals filled with Unionist symbolism. The mural of William of Orange's victory over the Catholic King James II (Battle of the Boyne, 1690)

thrills Unionist hearts. You'll find that one at the northern end of Sandy Row at the corner with Linfield Road.

TITANIC QUARTER

At its height, the Belfast shipyards employed more than 30,000 people. But after World War II, with the advent of air travel and the rise of cheaper labor at shipyards located in Asia, shipbuilding declined here and moved to other parts of the world. The last ocean liner was built here in 1961 and the very last ship of any kind built here sailed away in 2003. The shipyards continually downsized; some were abandoned while others morphed into repair yards for other maritime endeavors like oil-rig and oceanic wind-turbine repair.

By the mid-1990s, the proud former shipbuilding district along the River Lagan was a barren industrial wasteland. But during the Celtic Tiger boom years (which spilled over into the North), shrewd investors saw the real-estate potential and began building posh, high-rise condos.

The first landmark project to be completed was the Odyssey entertainment complex (in 2000). To draw more visitors and commemorate the proud shipbuilding industry of the Victorian and Edwardian ages, another flagship attraction was needed. The 100th anniversary of the *Titanic* disaster in 2012 provided the perfect opportunity, and the result was the Titanic Belfast Museum, a phenomenally popular exhibition about the ill-fated ship. Today, the entire eastern bank of the Lagan is a riverfront promenade nicknamed "the Maritime Mile" and is a delightful walk (described later).

While you can just go the Titanic Belfast Museum, if you have time, see the museum as part of my walk. The slick new Glider tram #G2 from City Hall makes stops all along the way, including at the Titanic Belfast Museum and the HMS *Caroline*.

▲▲Titanic Quarter Walk

This self-guided walk takes about an hour, not including its two

BELFAST

major stops: the Titanic Belfast Museum and the HMS *Caroline* (both described later).

• *Belfast's leaning* ❶ **Albert Memorial Clock Tower** *marks the start of this walk (for more about the clock tower, see page 73). From there, head for the River Lagan, where you'll find the...*

❷ Lagan Weir

The first step in rejuvenating a derelict riverfront is to tame the river, get rid of the tides, and build modern embankments. The star of that major investment is the Lagan Weir, the people-friendly gateway to the Titanic Quarter. Built in 1994, the weir is made up of four large pier houses and five giant gates that divide freshwater from saltwater and control the river's flow—no more flooding. You can walk across the weir on a curving pedestrian footbridge (added in 2015). Notice how much lower the water is on the saltwater side of the weir (depending on the tide). Looking downstream, on the left stands a glassy high-rise apartment building—the tallest in all of Ireland. Moored below that is the funky harbor tour boat (described earlier, under "Tours in Belfast"). On the other side, a popular riverside walk goes scenically inland from here 14 miles along the old tow path.

• *Cross the weir and turn left.*

❸ Maritime Mile Walk

This parklike promenade laces together several sights along the riverbank. It's lined with historic photo plaques that tell the story

of this industrial river. The far side of the river was busy with trade (importing and exporting) and this side was all about shipbuilding. All along the way you'll get glimpses (to the right) of the city's iconic and giant yellow cranes. The big *H&W* stands for Harland and Wolff, Belfast's once mighty shipyard, but locals

just call them Samson and Goliath. (In 2019, the last 130 employees of Harland and Wolf saw their once proud company file for bankruptcy.)

Today, shipbuilding is the stuff of museums; this riverbank is all about entertainment and tourism. Find a *Game of Thrones* stained-glass window. You'll see a couple of these on this walk. (Belfast has six, commemorating the TV series filmed here that gave tourism in Northern Ireland a nice bump.)

• *Continue walking until you reach the Odyssey arena complex.*

BELFAST

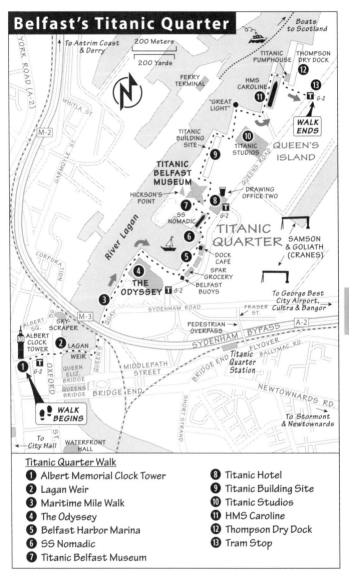

Belfast's Titanic Quarter

Boats to Scotland

To Antrim Coast & Derry

200 Meters
200 Yards

YORK ROAD (A-2)

WHITLA ST.

M-2

GARMOYLE ST.

FERRY TERMINAL

TITANIC PUMPHOUSE

THOMPSON DRY DOCK

⑫

HMS CAROLINE

⑬ T G-2

⑪

"GREAT LIGHT"

WALK ENDS

TITANIC BUILDING SITE

⑩
TITANIC STUDIOS

QUEEN'S ISLAND

⑨

QUEENS ROAD

TITANIC BELFAST MUSEUM

HICKSON'S POINT

⑦

⑧ T G-2

DRAWING OFFICE TWO

SS NOMADIC

River Lagan

⑥

CORPORATION

⑤

TITANIC QUARTER

SAMSON & GOLIATH (CRANES)

DOCK CAFÉ

SPAR GROCERY

BELFAST BUOYS

④
THE ODYSSEY T G-2

③

To George Best City Airport, Cultra & Bangor

SYDENHAM ROAD

FRASER ST.

A-2

M-3

QUAY

ALBERT SQ.

SKY-SCRAPER

ALBERT CLOCK TOWER

② LAGAN WEIR

① T G-2

QUEEN ELIZ. BRIDGE

QUEENS BRIDGE

OXFORD ST.

QUEENS QUAY

MIDDLEPATH STREET

BRIDGE END

PEDESTRIAN OVERPASS

SYDENHAM BYPASS

BRIDGE END FLYOVER

BALLYMAC. RD.

Titanic Quarter Station

NEWTOWNARDS RD.

SHORT STRAND

WALK BEGINS

To City Hall

WATERFRONT HALL

To Stormont & Newtownards

BELFAST

Titanic Quarter Walk

① Albert Memorial Clock Tower
② Lagan Weir
③ Maritime Mile Walk
④ The Odyssey
⑤ Belfast Harbor Marina
⑥ SS Nomadic
⑦ Titanic Belfast Museum
⑧ Titanic Hotel
⑨ Titanic Building Site
⑩ Titanic Studios
⑪ HMS Caroline
⑫ Thompson Dry Dock
⑬ Tram Stop

❹ The Odyssey

This huge millennium-project complex offers a food pavilion, bowling alley, 12-screen cinema, and the **W5 science center** with interactive, educational exhibits for youngsters. Where else can a kid play a harp with laser-light strings? The "W5" stands for "who, what, when, where, and why" (£10, Mon-Sat 10:00-18:00, Sun from 12:00, 2 Queen's Quay, tel. 028/9046-7790, www.w5online. co.uk).

There's also the 12,000-seat **SSE Odyssey Arena,** where the Belfast Giants professional hockey team skates. The arena is all about boosting nonsectarian sports (like hockey) rather than traditionally Loyalist (cricket, rugby, soccer) or Republican (hurling, Gaelic football) sports that amp up anger between the tribes here. Under one giant roof, the entire city gets together—Loyalists and Republicans alike—and roots for the same team (hockey tickets from £20, Fri-Sat evenings Sept-March, tel. 028/9073-9074, www.belfastgiants.com).

• *Turning inland, you come to the* ❺ **Belfast Harbor Marina** *with an arc of shops and condos. On the corner are three huge buoys (buoy is pronounced "boy" in Britain). "The Belfast Buoys" (fondly called Tom, Dick, and Harry here) are described on info boards.*

At the far end of the arc of shops, find the **Dock Café,** a welcoming, convivial, and homey spot. Volunteer-run by local churches, its mission is to celebrate tolerance and "love your neighbor"—even if they practice a different religion. The coffee and cakes are wonderful, and you famously pay whatever you like at the "honesty box." There's soup and bread at lunch time (Mon-Sat 11:00-17:00, closed Sun). You're welcome to bring in a picnic from the adjacent SPAR grocery. Browsing the café's exhibits and displays and talking with its volunteers just makes you feel good here in a city with such a difficult story.

• *Ahead looms the superstar of the Titanic Quarter, the Titanic Belfast Museum with its striking white-and-gray building—as tall as the mighty ship itself. As you approach, you'll pass a big ship that was just the tender (the shuttle dinghy) for the* Titanic.

❻ SS *Nomadic*

This ship once ferried first-class passengers between the dock and the *Titanic*. Sitting in the dry dock where it was built, it's restored to appear as it was in 1912 when it ferried Benjamin Guggenheim, John Jacob Astor, Molly Brown, and Kate Winslet to that fateful voyage (50 yards south of the Titanic Belfast Museum, same hours and ticket as the museum). Nearby is **Hickson's Point,** a small building that was originally a chapel, built to provide a space for reflection for visitors to the *Titanic* exhibit. That was expecting a bit much from the tourists—no one used it, and now it's a pub.

• *Now is a good time to tour the* ❼ **Titanic Belfast Museum** *(see listing later in this section). Afterwards walk across the plaza to the...*

❽ Titanic Hotel

Housed in the former Harland and Wolff shipyard headquarters (known as the Drawing Office), this new hotel was permitted on condition that the public would be allowed to wander through its historic spaces. For 150 years, many of the largest and finest ships in the world were designed here. Now it's a classy hotel. Pick up an info sheet at the reception and treat the place like a free museum. *Titanic* aficionados and maritime design geeks love the place. The well-lit central space, now the Drawing Office Two pub, is where the plans for the *Titanic* were drawn.

• *Head for the river to see the place where the* Titanic *was actually built.*

❾ *Titanic* Building Site

A big, stylized **map** in the pavement shows the route of the *Titanic*'s one and only voyage. The brown benches are long and short—set up in dots and dashes to represent the Morse code distress transmissions sent on that fateful day. Just beyond two dashes, a few steps to the left, find the symbolic steel tip of the ship in the pavement and stand there looking out. This was where the bow was; the lampposts (stretching 300 yards before you) mark the size of the ship built here. Fifty yards ahead is a memorial with the names of all who perished.

• *Walk to what would have been the stern of the* Titanic.

❿ Titanic Studios

The *Game of Thrones* stained-glass window here features the Iron Throne. (You've just got to get a selfie.) The giant warehouse-like

building to your right was once the shipyard's Paint Hall, and is now Titanic Studios (not open to public)—the soundstage where much of *Game of Thrones* was filmed. Farther along is the gracefully revolving "Great Light" from a 1920s lighthouse. It was moved here from a nearby island. (The info board enthralls lighthouse fans.)

• *Continue walking up the promenade to the...*

⓫ HMS *Caroline*

A WWI battleship that fought in the 1916 Battle of Jutland, the HMS *Caroline* is one of only three surviving Royal Navy ships from that war, and well worth exploring (tour described later). During World War II and later, the *Caroline* served as a headquarters and training ship until being decommissioned in 2011—the second-oldest ship in the Royal Navy's service.

• *Walking from the HMS Caroline away from the river toward the tram stop you'll pass the...*

⑫ Thompson Dry Dock

This is the massive dry dock where the *Titanic* last rested on dry land. The Edwardian pump house filled the dry dock with water—and emptied it—in record time (26 million gallons in one hour). Slipways rolled new hulls down a slope into the water, where they were then towed to a dry dock. It's here that the final outfitting was completed, adding extra weight before the final watertight launch. You can pay to go inside the pump room and descend into the dry dock to walk in the *Titanic*'s massive footprint (£5, daily 10:00-17:00, café, tel. 028/9073-7813, www.titanicsdock.com).

• *Across the street is a* ⑬ **tram stop.** *From here you can catch the Glider tram #G2 back to City Hall, retracing much of what you just walked past with nice views of cranes and harbor action as you glide.*

Titanic Quarter Sights
▲▲▲Titanic Belfast Museum

This £97 million attraction stands right next to the original slipways where the *Titanic* was built. Creative displays tell the tale of the famous ocean liner, proudly heralded as the largest man-made moving object of its time. The sight has no actual artifacts from the underwater wreck (out of respect for the fact that it's a mass grave). The artifacts on display are from local shipbuilding offices and personal collections.

Cost and Hours: £19, £11.50 Late Saver Ticket sold one hour before closing; daily June-Aug 8:30-19:00, April-May and Sept 9:00-18:00, Oct-March 10:00-17:00; audioguide-£4, but you get plenty of info without it; tel. 028/9076-6399, www.titanicbelfast.com. Early Riser Tickets for some morning slots (book online) can save up to 30 percent.

Crowd-Beating Tips: Book ahead online to get the entry time you want and avoid ticket lines. For fewer crowds, go early or late as big bus tours and cruise-ship excursions can clog the exhibits from 9:30-15:00.

Getting There: From the Albert Memorial Clock Tower at the edge of the Cathedral Quarter, it's a 10-minute walk: Follow my "Titanic Quarter Walk" (described earlier). From Donegall Square, take the Glider tram (#G2, 6/hour) or go by taxi (about £6).

Tours: The **Discovery Tour** explains the striking architecture of the Titanic Belfast Museum building and the adjacent slipways where the ship was built (£9, 1 hour, call ahead for tour times).

Eating: The ground floor includes a **$ Galley Express** (sandwich café) as well as **$$ Bistro 401** (a carvery-style restaurant). Choices nearby include the upscale **$$$ Drawing Office Two** pub, occupying the rooms where the ill-fated vessel was designed (across the lane in the Titanic Hotel), and the **$ Dock Café,** a church-run community center serving pay-what-you-like soup, bread, cake, and coffee (described in the walk).

Visiting the Museum: The spacey architecture of the Titanic Belfast Museum building is a landmark on the city's skyline. Six stories tall, it's clad in more than 3,000 sun-reflecting aluminum panels. Its four corners represent the bows of the many ships (most of which didn't sink) that were built in these yards during the industrial Golden Age of Belfast.

You'll follow a one-way route through the exhibit's nine galleries on six floors. Helpful "crew" (museum staff) are posted throughout to answer questions.

The "shipyard ride" near the beginning is a fun (if cheesy) five-minute experience. Six people share a gondola as you glide through a series of vignettes that attempt to capture what it was like to be a worker building the ship. (There can be a 20-minute wait—if short on time, I'd skip it and use my time more productively in the fascinating displays that follow.)

Continuing on, you'll find a big window overlooking the actual construction site (which you can visit after leaving the building). Next, you'll see exhibits on the construction, historic photographs, proud displays of the opulence on board, a recounting of the disaster (with Morse code transmissions sent after the ship hit the iceberg) and, in the 200-seat Discovery Theatre, the seven-minute *Titanic Beneath* video, with eerie footage of the actual wreckage sprouting countless "rusticles" 12,000 feet down on the ocean floor. Don't miss the see-through floor panels at the foot of the movie screen where the wreck passes slowly under your feet. The last escalator leaves you on the ground floor facing the back door of the center.

And what do the people of Belfast have to say about the ship they built that sank on her first voyage? "She was OK when she left."

▲HMS *Caroline*

Launched in 1914, the HMS *Caroline* is the sole surviving ship of the greatest naval battle of World War I—the Battle of Jutland in the North Sea. Despite being the bloodiest day in British naval

history, it's regarded as a victory over the German Navy, which never challenged Britain again. Follow the one-way route with the included audioguide. You'll start with a fascinating exhibit about the ship, which includes a 10-minute *Jutland Experience* video. Then you'll enter the actual ship, restored as if time stopped in 1916 (dinner is still on the table), and are free to explore from the torpedo exhibit to the thunderous engine room. Locals nicknamed the *Caroline* the "HMS *Never Budge*" because she's been moored here for decades—she finally was converted into a museum in 2016.

Cost and Hours: £13.50, daily 10:00-17:00; walk around the ship to the adjacent building—the old pump house for the Thompson Dry Dock—for tickets; Alexandra Dock, Queen's Road, www.nmrn.org.uk.

SOUTH BELFAST
▲Ulster Museum

This is Belfast's most venerable museum. It offers an earnest and occasionally thought-provoking look at the region's history, with a cross-section of local artifacts.

Cost and Hours: £5 suggested donation; Tue-Sun 10:00-17:00, closed Mon; south of downtown, in the Botanic Gardens on Stranmillis Road, tel. 028/9044-0000, www.nmni.com.

Visiting the Museum: The five-floor museum is pretty painless. Ride the elevator to the top floor and follow the spiraling exhibits downhill through various zones. The top two floors are dedicated to rotating art exhibits, the next floor down covers local nature, and the two below that focus on history. The ground floor covers the Troubles, and has a coffee shop and gift shop.

The Art Zone displays beautifully crafted fine crystal and china. In the Nature Zone, audiovisuals trace how the Ice Age affected the local landscape. Dinosaur skeletons lurk, stuffed wildlife play possum, and geology rocks. Kids will enjoy the interactive Discover History room.

After a peek at a pretty good mummy, check out the *Girona* treasure. Soggy bits of gold, silver, leather, and wood were salvaged from the Spanish Armada's shipwrecked *Girona*, lost off the Antrim Coast north of Belfast in 1588.

In the delicately worded History Zone, a highlight is the wall covered with antique text. On the left is the Ulster Covenant

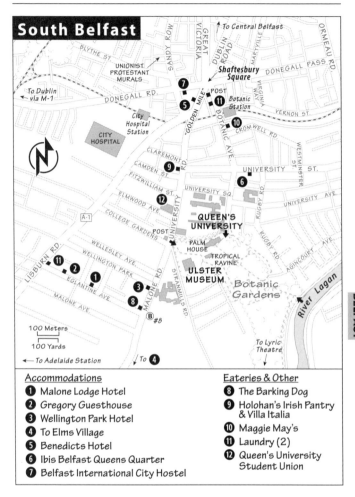

South Belfast

Accommodations
1. Malone Lodge Hotel
2. Gregory Guesthouse
3. Wellington Park Hotel
4. To Elms Village
5. Benedicts Hotel
6. Ibis Belfast Queens Quarter
7. Belfast International City Hostel

Eateries & Other
8. The Barking Dog
9. Holohan's Irish Pantry & Villa Italia
10. Maggie May's
11. Laundry (2)
12. Queen's University Student Union

(1912), signed in blood by Unionist Protestants to resist incorporation into an independent Irish state. On the right is the Irish Proclamation of the Republic (1916), dear to Nationalist Catholic hearts as the moral compass of the Easter Uprising. Compare the passion of these polar opposite points of view.

Then continue through the coverage of the modern-day Troubles as this museum strives for balanced and thought-provoking reflections. It's encouraging to see: When I first came to the North over 40 years ago, institutions like this would have only presented one point of view.

▲Botanic Gardens

This is the backyard of Queen's University, and on a sunny day, you couldn't imagine a more relaxing park setting. On a cold day, step

The Red Hand of Ulster

All over Belfast, you'll notice a curious symbol: a red hand facing you as if swearing a pledge or telling you to halt. You'll spot it, faded, above the Linen Hall Library door, in the wrought-iron fences of the Merchant Hotel, on old-fashioned clothes wringers (in the Ulster Folk Park and Transport Museum at Cultra), above the front door of a bank in Bangor, in the shape of a flowerbed at Mount Stewart House, in Loyalist paramilitary murals, on shield emblems in the gates of Republican memorials, and even on the flag of Northern Ireland (the white flag with the red cross of St. George). It's known as the Red Hand of Ulster—and it is one of the few emblems used by both communities in Northern Ireland.

Nationalists display a red hand on a yellow shield as a symbol of the ancient province of Ulster. It was the official crest of the once-dominant O'Neill clan (who fought tooth and nail against English rule) and today signifies resistance to British rule in these communities.

But you'll more often see the red hand in Unionist areas. They see it as a potent symbol of the political entity of Northern Ireland. The Ulster Volunteer Force chose it for their symbol in 1913 and embedded it in the center of the Northern Irish flag upon partition of the island in 1921. You may see the red hand clenched as a fist in Loyalist murals. One Loyalist paramilitary group even named itself the Red Hand Commandos.

The origin of the red hand comes from a mythological tale of two rival clans that raced by boat to claim a far shore. The first clan leader to touch the shore would win it for his people. Everyone aboard both vessels strained mightily at their oars, near exhaustion as they approached the shore. Finally, in desperation, the chieftain leader of the slower boat whipped out his sword and lopped off his right hand...which he then flung onto the shore, thus winning the coveted land. Moral of the story? The fearless folk of Ulster will do *whatever it takes* to get the job done.

into the Tropical Ravine for a jungle of heat and humidity. Take a quick walk through the Palm House, reminiscent of the one in London's Kew Gardens, but smaller. The Ulster Museum is on the garden's grounds.

Cost and Hours: Free; gardens daily 7:30 until dusk; Palm House daily 10:00-17:00, Oct-March until 16:00; tel. 028/9031-4762, www.belfastcity.gov.uk/parks.

Nearby: Just south of the gardens is the **Lyric Theatre,** an architecturally innovative building rebuilt in 2011 (no tours, but there are performances; see "Nightlife in Belfast," later).

BEYOND BELFAST
▲▲Ulster Folk Park and Transport Museum

This sprawling 180-acre, two-museum complex straddles the road and rail line at Cultra, midway between Bangor and Belfast (8 miles east of town).

Cost and Hours: £9 for each museum, £11 combo-ticket for both, £29 for families; March-Sept Tue-Sun 10:00-17:00; Oct-Feb Tue-Fri 10:00-16:00, Sat-Sun 11:00-16:00; closed Mon year-round; check the schedule for the day's special events, tel. 028/9042-8428, www.nmni.com.

Getting There: From Belfast, you can reach Cultra by taxi (£15), bus #502 (2/hour, 30 minutes, from Laganside Bus Centre), or train (2/hour, 15 minutes, from any Belfast train station or from Bangor). Buses stop right in the park, but schedules are skimpy on Saturday and Sunday. Train service is more dependable (and more frequent on the weekend): Get off at the Cultra stop.

Planning Your Time: Allow three hours, and expect lots of walking. Most people will spend an hour in the Transport Museum and a couple of hours at the Folk Park. You'll arrive (by rail or car) between the two museums a bit closer to the Transport Museum. From here, you have a choice of going downhill to the Transport Museum or 200 panting yards uphill into the Folk Park. Assess your energy level and plan accordingly. Those with a car can drive between the Transport Museum and the Folk Park (each has a parking lot), but as it is only 300 yards, it's simpler just to walk between them than to look for an open space on a busy day. Note that the Transport Museum is all indoors. The Folk Park involves more walking exposed to the elements between buildings spread across the upper hillside.

Visiting the Museums: The **Transport Museum** consists of three buildings. Start at the bottom and trace the evolution of transportation from 7,500 years ago—when people first decided to load an ox—to the first vertical takeoff jet. In 1909, the Belfast-based Shorts Aviation Company partnered with the Wright brothers to manufacture the first commercially available  aircraft. The middle building holds an intriguing section on the sinking of the *Titanic*. The top building covers the history of bikes, cars, and trains. The car section rumbles from the first car in Ireland (an 1898 Benz), through the "Cortina Culture" of the 1960s, to the local adventures of controversial automobile designer John DeLorean and a 1981 model of his sleek sports car.

The **Folk Park,** an open-air collection of 34 reconstructed buildings from all over the nine counties of Ulster, showcases the region's traditional lifestyles. After wandering through the old-town site (church, print shop, schoolhouse, humble Belfast row house, silent movie theater, and so on), you'll head off into the country to nip into cottages, farmhouses, and mills. Some houses are warmed by a wonderful peat fire and a friendly attendant. Your visit can be dull or vibrant, depending upon whether attendants are available to chat. Drop a peat brick on the fire.

▲Carrickfergus Castle

Built during the Norman invasion of the late 1100s, this historic castle stands sentry on the shore of Belfast Lough. William of

Orange landed here in 1690, when he began his Irish campaign against deposed King James II. In 1778, the American privateer ship *Ranger* (the first ever to fly the Stars and Stripes), under the command of John Paul Jones, defeated the HMS *Drake* just up the coast. These days the castle feels a bit sanitized and geared for kids, but it's an easy excursion if you're seeking a castle experience near the city.

Cost and Hours: £5.50; daily 9:00-17:00, Oct-March until 16:00; tel. 028/9335-1273.

Getting There: It's a 20-minute train ride from Belfast (on the line to Larne). Turn left as you exit the train station and walk straight downhill for five minutes—all the way to the waterfront—passing under the arch of the old town wall en route. You'll find the castle on your right.

▲The Gobbins Cliff Path

Newly reopened in 2016, the Gobbins Cliff Path is an Edwardian adventure with birds, beautiful scenery, and occasional rogue waves. Located 20 miles northeast of Belfast, beyond Carrickfergus, this complex path—a mix of tunnel bridges, railings, and steps carved, hammered, or fastened to the cliff—was first opened in 1902, designed to boost tourism. Once popular, it fell into disrepair during World War II and was closed for decades. The newly reinforced path (which, to spoil all the turn-of-the-century fun, now requires helmets and guides) takes two to three hours to hike, and is awkward and steep in places, but not terribly strenuous. You'll spot puffins, cormorants, and kittiwakes in nesting areas along the way.

Cost and Hours: £10, visitors center open daily 9:30-17:30, required guided hikes generally hourly (weather permitting), book in advance as tours can fill up, tel. 028/9337-2318, 68 Middle Road, Islandmagee, www.thegobbinscliffpath.com.

Getting There: By car, take the A-2 from Belfast to Larne, turn right on B-90, and follow signs to *Islandmagee* and *The Gobbins*. Without a car, take a train to Ballycarry (on the Larne line) and either walk a mile to the visitors center, or take a taxi (Ballycarry Cabs, tel. 028/9303-8131). McCombs Coach Tours may offer summer excursions here from Belfast, which will be the best connection for those without wheels—check their offerings by phone or online (tel. 028/9031-5333, www.mccombscoaches.com, info@mccombscoaches.com).

Nightlife in Belfast

Theater
Located beside the River Lagan (near Queen's University), the **Lyric Theatre** is a Belfast institution. Rebuilt in 2011, it represents the cultural rejuvenation of the city—the building was partially funded by donations from actors such as Liam Neeson, Kenneth Branagh, and Meryl Streep. While there are no public tours, it's a good place to see quality local productions (tickets £15-25, box office open daily 10:00-17:00, 55 Ridgeway Street, tel. 028/9038-1081, www.lyrictheatre.co.uk).

Traditional Music and Dance
Belfast Story features former *Riverdance* musicians and dancers in an energetic hour-long performance celebrating the people, poetry, and music of Belfast. It's held in a characteristic and recommended pub—with the local crowd on the ground floor and tourists packed into a tiny performance room upstairs (£25; May-Oct Fri-Sat at 20:00, upstairs in Madden's Pub at 74 Berry Street, mobile 079-7189-5746, www.belfasthiddentours.com, Conner Owens).

Musical Pub Crawl
Belfast Trad Trail Tours is led by two local musicians. You'll walk to three fun drinking establishments in the Cathedral Quarter, where they play and explain traditional Irish music. It's a great intro to Irish music and Belfast's pulsing evening scene (£15, 2.5 hours, mid-May-Aug Sat at 16:00, meet at Dirty Onion Pub, 3 Hill Street, tel. 028/9028-8818, www.tradtrail.com).

▲▲Live Music

A great way to connect with the people and culture of Belfast is over a beer in a pub. The first five pubs listed here have music—mostly traditional Irish (a.k.a. trad)—nearly every night. Four are near each other in the Cathedral Quarter. The Points Whiskey and Alehouse is farther south near the "Golden Mile"/Great Victoria Street. Bert's, also in the Cathedral Quarter, is a slinky lounge for live jazz and cocktails. Check pub websites to see what's on when you're in town.

Kelly's Cellars, once a rebel hangout (see plaque above door), still has a very gritty Irish feel. It's 300 years old, has a great fun-loving energy inside, and a lively terrace (Mon-Sat 11:30-24:00, Sun 13:00-23:30; live music nightly at 21:30, trad music Tue-Thu and Sat-Sun at 21:30; 32 Bank Street, 100 yards behind Tesco supermarket, access via alley on left side when facing Tesco, tel. 028/9024-6058, www.facebook.com/kellys.

cellars). They only serve traditional Irish stew until 16:00 but you can bring in fish-and-chips from the corner joint (the recommended Manny's) any time.

Madden's Pub is wonderfully characteristic, with a local crowd and trad music every night from 21:00 (no food, also hosts the "Belfast Story" described earlier, 2 blocks from Kelly's Cellars at 74 Berry Street, tel. 028/9024-4114).

The John Hewitt is committed to the local arts scene—giving both musicians and artists a platform. They don't serve food but they do dish up live music almost nightly from 21:30 (trad music Tue and Sat-Sun, rock on Fri, folk and acoustic on Mon and Thu, closed Wed, 51 Donegall Street, tel. 028/9023-3768, www.thejohnhewitt.com).

The Duke of York is noisy for both eyes and ears—jammed with vintage mirrors and memorabilia, it feels like a drunken lamps-and-lighting store. They have live music nightly (from 21:30, often just one guitarist hollering above the din) to crank up the volume even more. It's on Commercial Court, the noisiest and most trendy/touristy street for nightlife in Belfast (7 Commercial Court, tel. 028/9024-1062, www.dukeofyorkbelfast.com).

The Points Whiskey and Alehouse is an authentic Belfast pub, famed for its music—trad and Irish rock on two stages nightly after 22:00. It's near Hotel Europa at 44 Dublin Road. They offer more music in the quieter and adjacent **An Síbín pub** (tel. 028/9099-4124, www.thepointsbelfast.com).

Bert's Jazz Bar, at the Merchant Hotel, is good if you're in the mood for a cocktail in a plush, velvety Art Deco lounge with live jazz (from 21:00 nightly, 16 Skipper Street, tel. 028/9026-2713).

Sleeping in Belfast

Belfast is more of a convention town than a tourist town, so business-class room rates are lower or soft on weekends. For cozy B&Bs, check out the Queen's University area or the nearby seaside town of Bangor.

CENTRAL BELFAST

To locate these hotels, see the "Central Belfast" map on page 70.

$$$$ Hotel Europa is Belfast's landmark hotel—fancy, comfortable, and central—with four stars and lower weekend rates. Modern yet elegant, this place is the choice of visiting diplomats (breakfast extra, Great Victoria Street, tel. 028/9027-1066, www. hastingshotels.com, res@eur.hastingshotels.com).

$$$ Jurys Inn, an American-style hotel that rents 190 identical modern rooms, is perfectly located two blocks from City Hall (breakfast extra, Fisherwick Place, tel. 028/9053-3500, www. jurysinns.com, jurysinnbelfast@jurysinns.com).

SOUTH BELFAST

To locate these hotels, see the "South Belfast" map on page 91.

South of Queen's University

Many of Belfast's best budget beds cluster in a comfortable, leafy neighborhood just south of Queen's University (near the Ulster Museum). The Botanic, Adelaide, and City Hospital **train stations** are nearby (I find Botanic the most convenient), and buses zip down Malone Road every 20 minutes. Any **bus** on Malone Road goes to Donegall Square East. **Taxis** take you downtown for about £6 (your host can call one).

Located directly across University Road from the red-brick university building, **Queen's University Student Union** is just as handy for tourists as it is for college students. Inside you'll find an ATM, WCs, a minimarket, and Wi-Fi. Grab a quick and cheap sandwich and coffee at **Clement's Coffee Shop** (closed Sun).

$$$$ Malone Lodge Hotel, by far the classiest listing in this neighborhood, provides slick, business-class comfort in 119 spacious rooms on a quiet street (elevator, restaurant, parking, 60 Eglantine Avenue, tel. 028/9038-8000, www.malonelodgehotel.com, info@malonelodgehotel.com).

$$$$ Gregory Guesthouse, with its stately red brick, ages gracefully behind a green lawn with 15 large, fresh rooms. Prices are soft, so it can be a good value with its subtle charm on a quiet street (family room, parking, 32 Eglantine Ave, tel. 028/9066-3454, www.thegregorybelfast.com, info@thegregorybelfast.com).

$$ Wellington Park Hotel is a dependable, if unimaginative, chain-style hotel with 75 rooms. It's predictable but in a good location (pay parking, 21 Malone Road, tel. 028/9038-1111, www.wellingtonparkhotel.com, info@wellingtonparkhotel.com).

¢ Elms Village, a huge Queen's University dorm complex, rents 100 basic, institutional rooms (all singles) to travelers during summer break (July and Aug only, coin-op laundry, self-serve kitchen; reception building is 50 yards down entry street, marked *Elms Village* on low brick wall, 78 Malone Road; tel. 028/9097-4525, www.stayatqueens.com, accommodation@qub.ac.uk).

Between Queen's University and Shaftesbury Square

$$$ Benedicts Hotel has 32 rooms in a good location at the northern fringe of the Queen's University district. Its popular bar is a maze of polished wood and can be loud on weekend nights (elevator, 7 Bradbury Place, tel. 028/9059-1999, www.benedictshotel.co.uk, info@benedictshotel.co.uk).

$$ Ibis Belfast Queens Quarter, part of a major European hotel chain, has 56 practical rooms in a convenient location. It's a great deal if you're not looking for cozy character (breakfast extra, elevator, a block north of Queen's University at 75 University Street, tel. 028/9033-3366, https://ibis.accorhotels.com, h7288@accor.com).

¢ Belfast International City Hostel, big and creatively run, provides the best value among Belfast's hostels. It's near Botanic Station, in the heart of the lively university district, and has 24-hour reception. Paul, the manager, is a veritable TI, with a passion for his work (private rooms available, 22 Donegall Road, tel. 028/9031-5435, www.hini.org.uk, info@hini.org.uk).

Eating in Belfast

CENTRAL BELFAST
For locations, see the "Central Belfast" map on page 70.

Fine Dining Near City Hall
$$$ The Ginger Bistro serves a smart local crowd Irish/Asian cuisine with special attention to vegetarian and fish dishes. The casual front is for walk-ins, and the quieter, more romantic back is for those with reservations (Tue-Sat 12:00-22:00, closed Sun-Mon, early-bird specials Tue-Fri until 18:45, 68 Great Victoria Street, tel. 028/9024-4421, www.gingerbistro.com).

\$\$\$ Yūgo Asian Fusion Food is a foodie fave, trendy but with no pretense and lots of booze. The small dining room is tight with a dozen tables; eating at the bar gets you a fun view of the open kitchen. While they have main courses, their small plates—£5-10 each—are designed to be eaten tapas style (vegetarian-friendly, Tue-Sat 12:00-15:00 & 17:00-22:00, closed Sun-Mon, reservations smart, 3 Wellington Street, tel. 028/9031-9715, www.yugobelfast.com).

\$\$\$ Deanes Love Fish and **Deanes Meatlocker** are side-by-side sister places run by the powerhouse restaurateur of Deanes Eipic, a Michelin-star place next door. Each has a confident, impersonal vibe with good-value meals in a classy atmosphere; the lunch and pre-theater specials are especially economic. I prefer the Loves Fish place with its minimalist, nautical feel. The Meatlocker is more for red meat and romance (Mon-Sat 12:00-15:00 & 17:00-22:00, closed Sun, one block from City Hall at 28 Howard Street, tel. 028/9033-1134, www.michaeldeane.co.uk).

\$\$\$ Café Parisien serves French dishes with a classy *Titanic* (and peaceful blues) ambience. It's in a great central location with a terrace looking directly at City Hall—especially nice when dining outdoors (Mon-Fri 11:30-16:00 & 17:00-22:30, Sat-Sun 12:00-22:30, evening reservations smart; a few doors east of the TI on Donegall Square North, tel. 028/9590-4338, www.cafeparisienbelfast.com).

Other Options Near City Hall

\$\$\$ Coco Restaurant is a spacious place with a quirky sense of style, serving reliably tasty modern Irish and Continental dishes (nightly from 17:30, good early-bird specials until 19:00, a couple of blocks behind City Hall at 7 Linen Hall Street, tel. 028/9031-1150, Tim).

\$\$ Crown Liquor Saloon and Dining Room is a dazzling gin palace on every sightseers list. The ground floor pub is a mesmerizing mishmash of mosaics and shareable snugs (booths—best to reserve), topped with a smoky tin ceiling. The dining room upstairs is similarly elegant but much quieter. Both serve the same pub grub but upstairs seating comes with  table service (downstairs 11:30-20:00, upstairs 12:30-22:00, across from Hotel Europa at 46 Great Victoria Street, tel. 028/9024-3187, www.nicholsonspubs.co.uk).

$$ Made in Belfast has a crazy, fake-bohemian dining room with a creative and fun-loving menu. While exciting a decade ago, it's a bit tired now, but I find the food inviting, the spacious seating enjoyable, and the lunch/early-bird specials (until 18:00) a good value (daily, on Wellington Street a block from City Hall, tel. 028/9024-6712). A second location with similar vibes and menu is in the Cathedral Quarter (facing the cathedral at 23 Talbot Street, tel. 028/9545-8120).

$$ The Morning Star is a well-worn, once-elegant eatery with a characteristic pub on the ground floor (serving a hearty £6 lunch buffet) and a low-energy dining hall upstairs. It has a good reputation for solid food in a historic pub (same pub-grub menu throughout, daily 12:00-22:00; down an alley just off High Street at 17 Pottinger's Entry, alley entry is roughly opposite the post office, tel. 028/9023-5986).

Cheap Lunches in City Hall: $ The **Bobbin Café** at City Hall is a good, cheap, and cheery little cafeteria serving soups, sandwiches, and hot dishes (daily 9:00-17:00, tel. 028/9050-2068). A nonprofit, they employ young people with learning disabilities.

Groceries: Small late-night corner grocery stores are all over town. The **Tesco Express** across from Hotel Europa is open very late and seems equipped for the hungry traveler.

Cathedral Quarter

In addition to the eateries listed here, there's a second location of Made in Belfast (see above).

$$$$ The Merchant Hotel presents its afternoon tea in an expensive ritual. You'll enjoy velvety Victorian splendor under an opulent dome with a piano accompaniment.

Sit under the biggest chandelier in Northern Ireland as you dine in the great hall of a former bank headquarters. If you've got a little money to burn, consider dressing up the best you can and indulging. You'll go home with a fancy box of leftovers (£30/person, daily 12:30-16:30, reservations smart, 35 Waring Street, tel. 028/9023-4888, www.themerchanthotel.com). Dinner is less expensive (daily 17:30-21:45, mod Irish/French cuisine).

$$$ Bert's Jazz Bar, also at the Merchant Hotel, is a fine option if you're looking for French cuisine served with jazz. Their early-bird special is a good value (daily generally 17:00-22:00, 16 Skipper Street, tel. 028/9026-2713).

$$ Fish City is a simple, peaceful dining room with an open kitchen, attentive service, spacious seating with nautical decor, and a focus on quality. Their seafood is caught under high environmental standards (daily 12:00-21:00, 33 Ann Street, tel. 028/9023-1000, Grace).

$$$ Ox Cave is a sleek and mod place with aproned French elegance. It was designed by the owners of the adjacent Michelin-starred Ox restaurant to entertain diners with wine and cheese as they wait for their table. But with charming Alain as your host, you could settle in here to make a meal from their charcuterie and cheese plates and exciting wines. Have fun with their wine matrix—lots of vintages by the glass at the same price (Tue-Sat 16:00 until late, closed Sun-Mon, 3 Oxford Street, tel. 028/9023-2567).

$$$$ The Muddlers Club, a loud, trendy, spacious, industrial-mod place, has an open kitchen and a fun format: a single, six-course, £55 fixed-price meal of international-style dishes that changes daily. Their wine-pairing option makes the tasting menu even better. Eating here is expensive, but it's a memorable slice of Belfast (Tue-Sat 17:30-22:00, closed Sun-Mon, Warehouse Lane off Waring Street, tel. 028/9031-3199).

$$$ Mourne Seafood Bar is my choice for seafood in an elegant setting with a fun staff and smart clientele. It's run by a marine biologist and a great chef—no gimmicks, just top-quality seafood (daily 12:00-21:30, reservations smart, 34 Bank Street, tel. 028/9024-8544, www.mourneseafood.com). As it's next to Kelly's Cellars (described earlier, under "Nightlife in Belfast"), consider dining here and then enjoying the music next door.

$ Manny's Chapel Lane Fish & Chips is a classic, cheap, neighborhood chippie. You're welcome to bring your fish down the block to Kelly's Cellars for a beer and to enjoy the music (closed Sun, 11 Chapel Lane, tel. 028/9031-9165).

$ The Yardbird, rough and spacious, is housed in an open-beam attic and serves a down-and-dirty menu of ribs and wings. It's known for its cheap and tasty rotisserie chicken (daily 12:00-22:00, 3 Hill Street, tel. 028/9024-3712). The **Dirty Onion** (downstairs) is a popular pub that spills suds and live music into its packed outer courtyard on summer nights.

NEAR QUEEN'S UNIVERSITY
For locations, see the "South Belfast" map on page 91.

$$$ The Barking Dog, elegant and inviting, serves small plates to be enjoyed family style, along with pastas and burgers. It's closest to my cluster of accommodations south of the university (daily 12:00-14:30 & 17:00-22:00, near corner of Eglantine Avenue at 33 Malone Road, tel. 028/9066-1885).

$$$ Holohan's Irish Pantry is like eating in a wealthy grandma's dining room. It's small with an inviting and nostalgic menu of Irish dishes—both classic and modern. The chef has a passion for seasonal ingredients (Tue-Sat 17:00-23:30, Sun 12:00-21:00, closed Mon, reservations smart, 43 University Road, tel. 028/9029-1103, www.holohanspantry.co.uk).

$$ **Villa Italia** packs in crowds hungry for linguini and *bistecca*. Huge and family-friendly, with checkered tablecloths and a wood-beamed ceiling draped with grape leaves, it's a little bit of Italy in Belfast (Mon-Sat 17:00-23:00, Sun 12:30-21:30, three long blocks south of Shaftesbury Square, at intersection with University Street, 39 University Road, tel. 028/9032-8356).

$$ **Maggie May's** serves hearty, simple, affordable meals in a tight and cheery little bistro room (Sun-Thu 8:00-22:00, Fri-Sat until 23:00, one block south of Botanic Station at 50 Botanic Avenue, tel. 028/9032-2662).

Belfast Connections

BY TRAIN OR BUS

For schedules and prices for trains and buses in Northern Ireland, check with Translink (tel. 028/9066-6630, www.translink.co.uk). Note that service is less frequent on Sundays.

From Belfast by Train to: Dublin (8/day, 2 hours), **Derry** (10/day, 2.5 hours), **Larne** (hourly, 1 hour), **Portrush** (15/day, 2 hours, transfer in Coleraine), **Bangor** (2/hour, 30 minutes).

By Bus to: Portrush (12/day, 2 hours; scenic-coast route, 2.5 hours), **Derry** (hourly, 2 hours), **Dublin** (hourly, most via Dublin Airport, 3 hours), **Galway** (every 2 hours, 5 hours, change in Dublin), **Glasgow** (3/day, 6 hours), **Edinburgh** (1/day direct, 2/day with change in Glasgow, 7-8 hours). The Europa Bus Centre is behind Hotel Europa (Ulsterbus tel. 028/9033-7003 for destinations in Scotland and England).

BY PLANE

Belfast has two airports. **George Best Belfast City Airport** (airport code: BHD, tel. 028/9093-9093, www.belfastcityairport.com) is a five-minute, £8 taxi ride from town (near the docks) or a £2.60 ride on the Airport Express bus #600 (hourly from Europa Bus Centre). Meanwhile, **Belfast International Airport** (airport code: BFS, tel. 028/9448-4848, www.belfastairport.com) is 18 miles west of town—an £8 ride on the Airport Express bus #300 (hourly from Europa Bus Centre next to Hotel Europa).

If you're headed for Edinburgh or Glasgow, flying is generally better than taking the ferry (slow and not that scenic), as it's a fairly cheap, short trip.

It's also fast, cheap, and easy to get to Belfast directly from **Dublin Airport.** The **Aircoach** express bus runs through the night in each direction (hourly, 2 hours). It stops at both Dublin Airport terminals and in downtown Belfast on Glengall Street (next to the Europa Hotel and Great Victoria Street station). With this service you can spend your last night in Belfast and fly out of Dublin in the morning (£14 from Belfast, €17 from Dublin, tel. 028/9033-0655, www.aircoach.ie).

BY FERRY

To Scotland: You can sail between Belfast and **Cairnryan** on the Stena Line ferry. A Rail Link coach connects the Cairnryan port to Ayr, where you'll catch a train to Glasgow Central station (6/day, 2.5 hours by ferry plus 2.5 hours by bus and train, tel. 028/9074-7747, www.stenaline.co.uk). The P&O Ferry (tel. 01304/448-888, www.poferries.com) goes from **Larne,** 20 miles north of Belfast, to **Cairnryan** (6/day, 2 hours), with bus or rail connections from there to Glasgow and Edinburgh. There are hourly trains between Belfast and Larne (1-hour trip, Larne TI tel. 028/2826-2495).

To England: You can sail from Belfast to **Liverpool** (generally 2/day, 8 hours, arrives in port of Birkenhead—10 minutes from Liverpool, tel. 028/9074-7747, www.stenaline.co.uk).

BELFAST

Bangor

To stay in a laid-back seaside hometown—with more comfort per pound—sleep 12 miles east of Belfast in Bangor (BANG-grr). With elegant old homes facing its spruced-up harbor and not even a hint of big-city Belfast, this town has appeal, and it's a handy alternative for travelers who find Belfast booked up by occasional conventions and conferences.

Formerly a Victorian resort and seaside escape from the big city nearby, Bangor now has a sleepy residential feeling. To visit two worthwhile sights near Bangor—the Somme Museum and Mount Stewart House—consider renting a car for the day at nearby George Best Belfast City Airport, a 15-minute train trip from Bangor.

GETTING THERE

Catch the train to Bangor from either Lanyon Place/Central or Great Victoria Street stations (2/hour, 30 minutes, go to the end of the line—don't get off at Bangor West). Consider stopping en route at Cultra (Ulster Folk Park and Transport Museum; see page 93). The journey gives you a good close-up look at the giant Belfast harbor cranes.

Orientation to Bangor

Tourist Information: Bangor's TI is in a stone tower house (from 1637) on the harborfront, a 10-minute walk from the train station (Mon-Fri 9:15-17:00, Sat from 10:00, Sun from 13:00 except closed Sun Sept-April, 34 Quay Street, tel. 028/9127-0069, www. discovernorthernireland.com, search for "Bangor Visitor Information Centre").

Helpful Hints: You'll find **Laundry Chute** at 2 Market Square, a block east of the train station, hidden next to a parking lot behind the post office—easiest access is from Main Street and up Market Street (Mon-Fri 9:00-17:30, Sat until 15:30, closed Sun, tel. 028/9146-5900). **Kare Cabs** provides local taxi service (tel. 028/9145-6777). So does **Bangor Cabs** (tel. 028/9145-6456).

Sights in Bangor

Walks

For sightseeing, your time is better spent in Belfast. But if you have time to burn in Bangor, enjoy a walk beside the water on the **Coastal Path,** which leads west out of town from the marina. A pleasant three-mile level walk along the water leads you to Crawfordsburn Country Park in the suburb of Helen's Bay. Hidden in the trees above Helen's Bay beach is Grey Point Fort, with its two WWI artillery bunkers guarding the shore (generally Sat-Sun 12:00-16:00, tel. 028/9082-3247). Allow 1.5 hours each way as you share the easy-to-follow and mostly paved trail with local joggers, dog walkers, and bikers.

For a shorter walk with views of the marina, head to the end of the **North Pier,** where you'll find a mosaic honoring a portion of the D-Day fleet that rendezvoused offshore in 1944, far from Nazi reconnaissance aircraft. Keep an eye out in the marina for Rose the seal. Little kids may enjoy the **Pickie Fun Park** next to the marina, with paddleboat swan rides and miniature golf. The **Bangor Castle** grounds are good for picnics, and include a peaceful walled garden (free, Mon-Thu 10:00-17:00, Fri-Sun until 18:00).

North Down Museum

This small museum covers local history, from monastic days to Viking raids to Victorian splendor. It's hidden on the grassy grounds behind City Hall, uphill and opposite from the train station.

Cost and Hours: Free, July-Aug daily 10:00-16:30; Sept-June

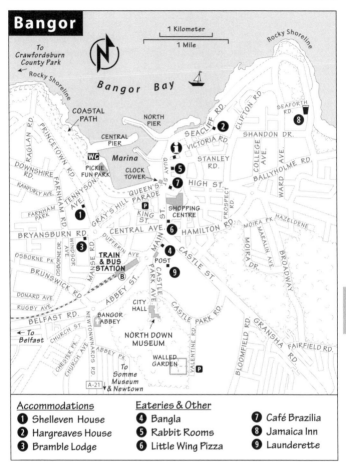

Bangor

To Crawfordsburn County Park

Bangor Bay

Rocky Shoreline

COASTAL PATH

NORTH PIER

CENTRAL PIER

Marina

WC

PICKIE FUN PARK

CLOCK TOWER

QUEEN'S PARADE

GRAY'S HILL

KING ST.

SHOPPING CENTRE

CENTRAL AVE.

BRYANSBURN RD.

TRAIN & BUS STATION

POST

ABBEY ST.

CITY HALL

BANGOR ABBEY

NORTH DOWN MUSEUM

WALLED GARDEN

To Somme Museum & Newtown

To Belfast

SEACLIFF RD.

VICTORIA RD.

STANLEY RD.

HIGH ST.

HAMILTON RD.

CASTLE ST.

CASTLE PARK RD.

CLIFTON RD.

SHANDON DR.

SEAFORTH RD.

COLLEGE AVE.

WARD AVE.

BALLYHOLME RD.

MOIRA PK.

HAZELDENE

MARALIN AVE.

BROADWAY

MOIRA DR.

BLOOMFIELD RD.

GRANSHA RD.

FAIRFIELD RD.

VALENTINE RD.

1 Kilometer

1 Mile

Accommodations
1 Shelleven House
2 Hargreaves House
3 Bramble Lodge

Eateries & Other
4 Bangla
5 Rabbit Rooms
6 Little Wing Pizza

7 Café Brazilia
8 Jamaica Inn
9 Launderette

Tue-Sat 10:00-16:30, Sun from 12:00, closed Mon; tel. 028/9127-1200, www.northdownmuseum.com.

NEAR BANGOR

The eastern fringe of Northern Ireland is populated mostly by people who consider themselves true-blue British citizens with a history of loyalty to the Crown that goes back more than 400 years. Two sights within reach by car from Bangor highlight this area's firm roots in British culture: the Somme Museum and Mount Stewart House. Call ahead to confirm sight opening hours.

Getting There: Bus service from Bangor is patchy (15 minutes to Somme Museum, one hour to Mount Stewart House with transfer, best to check schedule with Bangor TI or www.translink.co.uk). I'd rent a car instead at nearby George Best Belfast City

Airport, which is only 15 minutes by train from Bangor or 10 minutes from Belfast's Lanyon Place/Central Station. Because the airport is east of Belfast, your drive to these rural sights skips the headache of urban Belfast.

▲Mount Stewart House

No manor house in Ireland better illuminates the affluent lifestyle of the Protestant ascendancy than this lush estate. After the de-

feat of James II (the last Catholic king of England) at the Battle of the Boyne in 1690, the Protestant monarchy was in control—and the privileged status of landowners of the same faith was assured. In the 1700s, Ireland's many Catholic rebellions seemed finally to be squashed, so Anglican landlords felt safe flaunting their wealth in manor houses surrounded by utterly perfect gardens. The Mount Stewart House in particular was designed to dazzle.

Cost and Hours: £10.45 for house and gardens; house open daily 11:00-17:00, gardens from 10:00, closed Nov-Feb; 8 miles south of Bangor, just off A-20 beside Strangford Lough, tel. 028/4278-8387, www.nationaltrust.org.uk/mount-stewart.

Visiting the House: In the **manor house,** you'll glimpse the cushy life led by the Marquess of Londonderry and his heirs over the past three centuries. The main entry hall is a stunner, with a black-and-white checkerboard tile floor, marble columns, classical statues, and pink walls supporting a balcony with a domed ceiling and a fine chandelier. In the dining room, you'll see the original seats occupied by the rears of European heads of state, brought back from the Congress of Vienna after Napoleon's 1815 defeat.

A huge painting of Hambletonian, a prize-winning racehorse, hangs above the grand staircase, dwarfing a portrait of the Duke of Wellington in a hall nearby. The heroic duke (worried that his Irish birth would be seen as lower class by British blue bloods) once quipped in Parliament, "Just because one is born in a stable does not make him a horse." Irish emancipator Daniel O'Connell retorted, "Yes, but it could make you an ass."

Afterward, wander the expansive manicured **gardens.** The fantasy life of parasol-toting, upper-crust Victorian society seems to ooze from every viewpoint. Fanciful sculptures of extinct dodo birds and monkeys holding vases on their heads set off predictably classic Italian and Spanish sections. An Irish harp has been trimmed out of a hedge a few feet from a flowerbed shaped like the Red Hand of Ulster. Swans glide serenely among the lily pads on a small lake.

Somme Museum

World War I's trench warfare was a meat grinder. More British soldiers died in the last year of that war than in all of World War II. Northern Ireland's men were not spared—especially during the bloody Battle of the Somme in France, starting in July 1916 (see the "1916" sidebar on page 74). Among the Allied forces was the British Army's 36th Ulster Division, which drew heavily from this loyal heartland of Northern Ireland. The 36th Ulster Division suffered brutal losses at the Battle of the Somme—of the 760 men recruited from the Shankill Road area in Belfast, only 10 percent survived.

Exhibits portray the battle experience through a mix of military artifacts, photos, historical newsreels, and life-size figures posed in trench warfare re-creations. To access the majority of the exhibits, it's essential to take the one-hour guided tour (leaving hourly, on the hour). Visiting this place is a moving experience, but it can only hint at the horrific conditions endured by these soldiers.

Cost and Hours: £7; July-Aug Mon-Fri 10:00-17:00, Sat from 11:00, last tour one hour before closing, closed Fri Sept-June and Sun year-round; 3 miles south of Bangor just off A-21 at 233 Bangor Road, tel. 028/9182-3202, www.irishsoldier.org. A coffee shop is located at the center.

Sleeping in Bangor

Visitors arriving in Bangor (by train) come down Main Street, a 10-minute (mostly downhill) walk to reach the harbor marina. You'll find Hargreaves House up the east side of the harbor to the right, along the waterfront on Seacliff Road. The other two listings are to the left, closer to the train station and farther from the water. Take the first immediate left out of the station onto steeply downhill Dufferin Avenue; both are near the roundabout at the bottom.

$$$ Shelleven House is an old-fashioned, well-kept, stately place with 13 prim rooms on the quiet corner of Princetown Road and Tennyson Avenue (RS%, family rooms, parking, 61 Princetown Road, tel. 028/9127-1777, www.shellevenhouse.com, info@ shellevenhouse.com, Sue and Paul Toner).

$$ Hargreaves House, a homey Victorian waterfront ref-

BELFAST

uge with three cozy, refurbished rooms, is Bangor's best value, run by ever-helpful Pauline (RS%—use code "HHRS18," ocean views, parking, 15-minute walk from train station but worth it, 78 Seacliff Road, tel. 028/9146-4071, mobile 079-8058-5047, www. hargreaveshouse.com, info@hargreaveshouse.com).

$ Bramble Lodge is closest to the train station (10-minute walk), offering three inviting and spotless rooms (1 Bryansburn Road, tel. 028/9145-7924, mobile 077-9262-8001, jacquihanna_bramblelodge@yahoo.co.uk, Jacquiline Hanna).

Eating in Bangor

Most restaurants in town stop seating at about 20:30.

$$$ Bangla serves fine Indian cuisine with attentive service and a good-value early-bird option before 19:00 (daily 12:00-14:00 & 16:30-23:00, 115 Main Street, tel. 028/9127-1272).

$$ The **Rabbit Rooms** serves hearty Irish food to local crowds with live music after the dinner service several nights a week (daily 12:00-21:00, music Mon and Thu-Sat, near the harbor at 33 Quay Street, tel. 028/9146-7699).

$ Little Wing Pizza is a friendly joint serving tasty pizza, pasta, and salads. Grab your food to go and munch by the marina. It's also one of the few places in town that serves food later at night (daily 11:00-22:00, 37 Main Street, tel. 028/9147-2777).

$ Café Brazilia, a popular locals' lunch hangout with a simple menu, is across from the stubby clock tower (Mon-Sat 8:00-16:30, Sun from 10:00, 13 Bridge Street, tel. 028/9127-2763).

The **$$ Jamaica Inn** offers pleasant pub grub and a breezy waterfront porch (food served about 12:00-21:00, 10-minute walk east of the TI, 188 Seacliff Road, tel. 028/9147-1610).

PRACTICALITIES

This section covers just the basics on traveling in Northern Ireland (for much more information, see *Rick Steves Ireland*). You'll find free advice on specific topics at www.ricksteves.com/tips.

While it shares an island with the Republic of Ireland, Northern Ireland is part of the United Kingdom—which makes its currency, phone codes, and other practicalities different from the Republic.

MONEY

For currency, Northern Ireland uses the pound (£): 1 pound (£1) = about $1.30. One pound is broken into 100 pence (p). To convert prices in pounds to dollars, add about 30 percent: £20 = about $25, £50 = about $65. (Check www.oanda.com for the latest exchange rates.) While the pound used here is called the "Ulster Pound," it's interchangeable with the British pound.

The standard way for travelers to get local currency is to withdraw money from an ATM (which locals may call a "cash point") using a debit card, ideally with a Visa or MasterCard logo. To keep your cash, cards, and valuables safe, wear a money belt.

Before departing, call your bank or credit-card company: Confirm that your card(s) will work overseas, ask about international transaction fees, and alert them that you'll be making withdrawals in Europe. Also ask for the PIN number for your credit card—you may need it for Europe's "chip-and-PIN" payment machines. Allow time for your bank to mail your PIN to you.

European cards use chip-and-PIN technology (most chip cards issued in the US instead have a signature option). Some European card readers may generate a receipt for you to sign, while others may prompt you to enter your PIN (so it's important to know the code for each of your cards). US credit cards may not work at some self-service payment machines (transit-ticket kiosks, parking, etc.). If your card won't work, look for a cashier who can process the transaction manually—or pay in cash.

Dynamic Currency Conversion: If merchants or hoteliers offer to convert your purchase price into dollars (called dynamic currency conversion, or DCC), refuse this "service." You'll pay extra in fees for the expensive convenience of seeing your charge in dollars. If an ATM offers to "lock in" or "guarantee" your conversion rate, choose "proceed without conversion." Other prompts might state, "You can be charged in dollars: Press YES for dollars, NO for pounds." Always choose the local currency.

STAYING CONNECTED

The simplest solution is to bring your own device—mobile phone, tablet, or laptop—and use it just as you would at home (following the money-saving tips below).

To call Northern Ireland from a US or Canadian number: Whether you're phoning from a landline, your own mobile phone, or a Skype account, you're making an international call. Dial 011-44 and then 28 (Northern Ireland's area code, minus its initial zero), followed by the local number. (The 011 is our international access code, and 44 is the UK's country code.) If dialing from a mobile phone, you can enter + in place of the international access code—press and hold the 0 key.

To call Northern Ireland from a European country: Dial 00-44 followed by 28 and the local number. (The 00 is Europe's international access code.)

To call within Northern Ireland and the UK: All of Northern Ireland shares one area code (028), making all calls within the country local—so you can leave off the area code and simply dial the local number if you're dialing from a local landline. But if you're calling from a mobile phone, or to or from elsewhere in the UK, you need to include the area code.

To call from Northern Ireland to another country: Dial 00 followed by the country code (for example, 1 for the US or Canada), then the area code and number. If you're calling European countries whose phone numbers begin with 0, you'll usually have to omit that 0 when you dial.

Tips: If you bring your own mobile phone, consider signing up for an international plan; most providers offer a global calling plan that cuts the per-minute cost of phone calls and texts, and a flat-fee data plan.

Use Wi-Fi whenever possible. Most hotels and many cafés offer free Wi-Fi, and you'll likely also find it at tourist information offices, major museums, and public-transit hubs. With Wi-Fi you

Sleep Code

Hotels are classified based on the average price of a typical en suite double room with breakfast in high season.

$$$$	**Splurge:**	Most rooms over £140
$$$	**Expensive:**	£110-140
$$	**Moderate:**	£80-110
$	**Budget:**	£50-80
¢	**Backpacker:**	Under £50
RS%	**Rick Steves discount**	

Unless otherwise noted, credit cards are accepted and free Wi-Fi is available. Comparison-shop by checking prices at several hotels (on each hotel's own website, on a booking site, or by email). For the best deal, *book directly with the hotel.* If the listing includes **RS%,** request a Rick Steves discount.

can use your phone or tablet to make free or inexpensive domestic and international calls via a calling app such as Skype, FaceTime, or Google Hangouts. When you can't find Wi-Fi, you can use your cellular network to connect to the Internet, send texts, or make voice calls. When you're done, avoid further charges by manually switching off "data roaming" or "cellular data."

It's generally not possible to dial UK toll or toll-free numbers from a US mobile or landline (although you can sometimes get through using Skype). Look for a direct-dial number instead.

Without a mobile device, you can make calls from your hotel and get online using public computers (there's usually one in your hotel lobby or at local libraries). Most hotels charge a high fee for international calls—ask for rates before you dial.

For more on phoning, see www.ricksteves.com/phoning. For a one-hour talk on "Traveling with a Mobile Device," see www.ricksteves.com/travel-talks.

SLEEPING

I've categorized my recommended accommodations based on price, indicated with a dollar-sign rating (see sidebar). I recommend reserving rooms in advance, particularly during peak season. Once your dates are set, check the specific price for your preferred stay at several hotels. You can do this either by comparing prices on Hotels.com, Booking.com, or the hotels' own websites. After you've zeroed in on your choice, book directly with the hotel itself. Contact small family-run hotels directly by phone or email: When you go direct instead of through a website, the owner avoids any third-party commission, giving them wiggle room to offer you a discount, a nicer room, or free breakfast. If you prefer to book online or are considering a hotel chain, it's to your advantage to use the hotel's website.

Restaurant Price Code

I've assigned each eatery a price category, based on the average cost of a typical main course. Drinks, desserts, and splurge items (steak and seafood) can raise the price considerably.

$$$$	**Splurge:**	Most main courses over £20
$$$	**Pricier:**	£15-20
$$	**Moderate:**	£10-15
$	**Budget:**	Under £10

In Northern Ireland, carryout fish-and-chips and other takeout food is **$**; a basic pub or sit-down eatery is **$$**; a gastropub or casual but more upscale restaurant is **$$$**; and a swanky splurge is **$$$$**.

For complicated requests, send an email with the following information: number and type of rooms; number of nights; arrival date; departure date; and any special requests. Hoteliers typically ask for your credit-card number as a deposit. The prices I list include a hearty breakfast (unless otherwise noted).

Know the terminology: An "en suite" room has a bathroom (toilet and shower/tub) actually inside the room; a room with a "private bathroom" can mean that the bathroom is all yours, but it's across the hall. A "standard" room could have two meanings. Big hotels in the UK sometimes call a basic en-suite room a "standard" room to differentiate it from a fancier "superior" or "deluxe" room. At small hotels and B&Bs, guests in a "standard" room have access to a bathroom that's shared with other rooms and down the hall.

Some hotels extend a discount to those who pay cash or stay longer than three nights. And some accommodations offer a special discount for Rick Steves readers, indicated in this guidebook by the abbreviation **"RS%."**

Compared to hotels, bed-and-breakfast places give you double the cultural intimacy for half the price. Many B&Bs take credit cards but may add the card service fee to your bill (about 3 percent). If you'll need to pay cash for your room, plan ahead.

A short-term rental—whether an apartment, house, or room in a local's home—is an increasingly popular alternative, especially if you plan to settle in one location for several nights. Websites such as Airbnb, FlipKey, Booking.com, and the HomeAway family of sites (HomeAway, VRBO, and VacationRentals) let you browse a wide range of properties.

EATING

I've categorized my recommended eateries based on price, indicated with a dollar-sign rating (see sidebar). The traditional "Ulster

Fry" breakfast includes juice, tea or coffee, cereal, eggs, bacon, sausage, toast, a grilled tomato, sautéed mushrooms, and black pudding. If that's too much for you, order only the items you want.

To dine affordably at classier restaurants, look for "early-bird specials" (offered about 17:30–19:00, last order by 19:00).

Smart travelers use pubs (short for "public houses") to eat, drink, and make new friends. Pub grub is Northern Ireland's best eating value. For about $15–20, you'll get a basic hot lunch or dinner. The menu is hearty and traditional: stews, soups, fish-and-chips, meat, cabbage, potatoes, and—in coastal areas—fresh seafood. Order drinks and meals at the bar, and pay as you order. Pubs that are attached to restaurants, advertise their food, and are crowded with locals are more likely to have fresh food and a chef than sell lousy microwaved snacks.

Most pubs have lagers (cold, refreshing, American-style beer), ales (amber-colored, cellar-temperature beer), bitters (hop-flavored ale, perhaps the most typical British beer), and stouts (dark and somewhat bitter—the most famous is Guinness, of course).

Tipping: At a sit-down place with table service, tip about 10 percent—unless the service charge is already listed on the bill. At pubs where you order food at the counter, a tip is not expected but is appreciated.

TRANSPORTATION

By Car: A car is a worthless headache in Belfast. But if venturing into the countryside, I enjoy the freedom of a rental car for reaching far-flung rural sights. It's cheaper to arrange most car rentals from the US. For route planning, consult www.viamichelin.com, and for tips on your car insurance options, see www.ricksteves.com/cdw (if you're also going to the Republic of Ireland, note that many credit-card companies do not offer collision coverage for rentals in the Republic). Bring your driver's license. On an all-Ireland trip, you can drive your rental car from Northern Ireland into the Republic of Ireland, but there may be a drop-off charge (as much as $150-200) if you return it in the Republic.

Some companies in Northern Ireland won't rent to anyone over 69. In the Republic of Ireland, you generally can't rent a car if you're 75 or older (unless you have a note from your doctor), and you'll usually pay extra if you're 70-74. In Northern Ireland, the speed limit is in miles per hour; in the Republic, it's in kilometers per hour.

Remember that people throughout Ireland drive on the left side of the road (and the driver sits on the right side of the car). You'll quickly master the many roundabouts: Traffic moves clockwise, cars inside the roundabout have the right-of-way, and entering traffic yields (look to your right as you merge). Note that "camera cops" strictly enforce speed limits by automatically snapping photos of speeders' license plates, then mailing them a bill. Also be aware that your US credit and debit cards with a chip may not work at self-service gas pumps and automated parking garages, but if you know your PIN, try it anyway. The easiest solution is carrying sufficient cash.

Local road etiquette is similar to that in the US. Ask your car-rental company for details, or check the US State Department website (www.travel.state.gov, select "International Travel," search for your country in the "Learn about your destination" box, then click on "Travel and Transportation").

By Train and Bus: You can check train and bus schedules at www.translink.co.uk, or call 028/9066-6630. To see if a rail pass could save you money, check www.ricksteves.com/rail. Long-distance buses (called "coaches") are about a third slower than trains, but they're also much cheaper. Bus stations are normally at or near train stations.

HELPFUL HINTS

Emergency Help: For any emergency service—ambulance, police, or fire—call **112** from a mobile phone or landline. For passport problems, call the **US Consulate** (in Belfast, tel. 028/9038-6100, after-hours emergency mobile 012-5350-1106, http://uk.usembassy. gov/embassy-consulates/belfast). The **Canadian Consulate** in Belfast (tel. 028/9754-2405) doesn't offer passport services; instead contact the Canadian High Commission in London (tel. 020/7004-6000, www.unitedkingdom.gc.ca). For other concerns, get advice from your hotel.

Theft or Loss: To replace a passport, you'll need to go in person to an embassy or consulate (see above). Cancel and replace your credit and debit cards by calling these 24-hour US numbers with a mobile phone: Visa (tel. +1 303/967-1096), MasterCard (tel. +1 636/722-7111), and American Express (tel. +1 336/393-1111). From a landline, you can call these US numbers collect by going through a local operator. File a police report either on the spot or within a day or two; you'll need it to submit an insurance claim for lost or stolen rail passes or travel gear, and it can help with replacing your passport or electronics. For more information, see www.ricksteves. com/help.

Time: Northern Ireland uses the 24-hour clock. It's the same through 12:00 noon, then keep going: 13:00, 14:00, and so on. Ireland, like Great Britain, is five/eight hours ahead of the East/West Coasts of the US (and one hour earlier than most of continental Europe).

Holidays and Festivals: Northern Ireland celebrates many holidays, which can close sights and attract crowds (book hotel rooms ahead). For information on holidays and festivals, check Northern Ireland's tourism website: www.discovernorthernireland.com. For a simple list showing major events, see www.ricksteves.com/festivals.

Numbers and Stumblers: What Americans call the second floor of a building is the first floor in Northern Ireland. Local people write dates as day/month/year, so Christmas 2021 is 25/12/21. For most measurements, Northern Ireland uses the metric system: A kilogram is 2.2 pounds, and a liter is about a quart. For driving distances, they use miles.

RESOURCES FROM RICK STEVES

This Snapshot guide is excerpted from my latest edition of *Rick Steves Ireland,* one of many titles in my ever-expanding series of guidebooks on European travel. I also produce a public television series, *Rick Steves' Europe,* and a public radio show, *Travel with Rick Steves.* My website, www.ricksteves.com, offers free travel information, a forum for travelers' comments, guidebook updates, my travel blog, an online travel store, and information on European rail passes and our tours of Europe. If you're bringing a mobile device, my free Rick Steves Audio Europe app features dozens of self-guided audio tours of the top sights in Europe, and travel interviews about Ireland. For more information, see www.ricksteves.com/audioeurope.

ADDITIONAL RESOURCES

Northern Ireland Tourist Information: www.discovernorthernireland.com
Passports and Red Tape: www.travel.state.gov
Packing List: www.ricksteves.com/packing
Travel Insurance: www.ricksteves.com/insurance
Cheap Flights: www.kayak.com or www.google.com/flights
Airplane Carry-on Restrictions: www.tsa.gov
Updates for This Book: www.ricksteves.com/update

HOW WAS YOUR TRIP?

To share your tips, concerns, and discoveries after using this book, please fill out the survey at www.ricksteves.com/feedback. Thanks in advance—it helps a lot.

PRACTICALITIES

INDEX

INDEX

Our website enhances this book and turns

Explore Europe

At rickstevens.com you can browse through thousands of articles, videos, photos and radio interviews, plus find a wealth of money-saving travel tips for planning your dream trip. And with our mobile-friendly website, you can easily access all this great travel information anywhere you go.

TV Shows

Preview the places you'll visit by watching entire half-hour episodes of *Rick Steves' Europe* (choose from all 100 shows) on-demand, for free.

your travel dreams into affordable reality

Radio Interviews

Enjoy ready access to Rick's vast library of radio interviews covering travel tips and cultural insights that relate specifically to your Europe travel plans.

Travel Forums

Learn, ask, share! Our online community of savvy travelers is a great resource for first-time travelers to Europe, as well as seasoned pros.

Travel News

Subscribe to our free Travel News e-newsletter, and get monthly updates from Rick on what's happening in Europe.

Classroom Europe

Check out our free resource for educators with 400+ short video clips from the *Rick Steves' Europe* TV show.

Rick's Free Travel App

Get your FREE **Rick Steves Audio Europe™** app to enjoy...

- Dozens of self-guided tours of Europe's top museums, sights and historic walks
- Hundreds of tracks filled with cultural insights and sightseeing tips from Rick's radio interviews
- All organized into handy geographic playlists
- For Apple and Android

With Rick whispering in your ear, Europe gets even better.

Find out more at ricksteves.com

Gear up for your next adventure at ricksteves.com

Light Luggage

Pack light and right with Rick Steves' affordable, custom-designed rolling carry-on bags, backpacks, day packs and shoulder bags.

Accessories

From packing cubes to moneybelts and beyond, Rick has personally selected the travel goodies that will help your trip go smoother.

Shop at ricksteves.com

Rick Steves has

Experience maximum Europe

Save time and energy

This guidebook is your independent-travel toolkit. But for all it delivers, it's still up to you to devote the time and energy it takes to manage the preparation and logistics that are essential for a happy trip. If that's a hassle, there's a solution.

Rick Steves Tours

A Rick Steves tour takes you to Europe's most interesting places with great

with minimum stress

guides and small groups of 28 or less. We follow Rick's favorite itineraries, ride in comfy buses, stay in family-run hotels, and bring you intimately close to the Europe you've traveled so far to see. Most importantly, we take away the logistical headaches so you can focus on the fun.

Join the fun

This year we'll take 33,000 free-spirited travelers— nearly half of them repeat customers—along with us on 50 different itineraries, from Athens to Istanbul. Is a Rick Steves tour the right fit for your travel dreams?

Find out at ricksteves.com, where you can also request Rick's latest tour catalog. Europe is best experienced with happy travel partners. We hope you can join us.

See our itineraries at ricksteves.com

A Guide for Every Trip

BEST OF GUIDES

Full-color guides in an easy-to-scan format. Focused on top sights and experiences in the most popular European destinations

Best of England
Best of Europe
Best of France
Best of Germany
Best of Ireland
Best of Italy
Best of Scotland
Best of Spain

COMPREHENSIVE GUIDES

City, country, and regional guides printed on Bible-thin paper. Packe[d] with detailed coverage for a multi[-] week trip exploring iconic sights and venturing off the beaten path

Amsterdam & the Netherlands
Barcelona
Belgium: Bruges, Brussels,
  Antwerp & Ghent
Berlin
Budapest
Croatia & Slovenia
Eastern Europe
England
Florence & Tuscany
France
Germany
Great Britain
Greece: Athens & the Peloponnese
Iceland
Ireland
Istanbul
Italy
London
Paris
Portugal
Prague & the Czech Republic
Provence & the French Riviera
Rome
Scandinavia
Scotland
Sicily
Spain
Switzerland
Venice
Vienna, Salzburg & Tirol

E BEST OF ROME

taly's capital, is studded with remnants and floodlit-fountain From the Vatican to the Colos-th crazy traffic in between, Rome rful, huge, and exhausting. The he heat, and the weighty history

of the Eternal City where Caesars walked can make tourists wilt. Recharge by tak-ing siestas, gelato breaks, and after-dark walks, strolling from one atmospheric square to another in the refreshing eve-ning air.

Credits

CONTRIBUTOR

Gene Openshaw

Gene has co-authored more than a dozen Rick Steves books, specializing in writing walks and tours of Europe's cities, museums, and cultural sights. He also contributes to Rick's public television series, produces tours for Rick Steves Audio Europe, and is a regular guest on Rick's public radio show. Outside of the travel world, Gene has co-authored *The Seattle Joke Book*. As a composer, Gene has written a full-length opera called *Matter*, a violin sonata, and dozens of songs. He lives near Seattle with his daughter, enjoys giving presentations on art and history, and roots for the Mariners in good times and bad.

ACKNOWLEDGMENTS

Thanks to Rozanne Stringer for her writing on the Celts, the Celtic Tiger, St. Brendan, and Irish art. Thanks also to Dave Fox of Globejotting.com for his writing on Guinness beer.

PHOTO CREDITS

Avalon Travel
Hachette Book Group
1700 Fourth Street
Berkeley, CA 94710

Printed in Canada by Friesens.
Sixth Edition, First printing February 2020.

ISBN 978-1-64171-220-0

For the latest on Rick's talks, guidebooks, tours, public television series, and public radio show, contact Rick Steves' Europe, 130 Fourth Avenue North, Edmonds, WA 98020, tel. 425/771-8303, www.ricksteves.com, rick@ricksteves.com.

The publisher is not responsible for websites (or their content) that are not owned by the publisher.

Rick Steves' Europe

Managing Editor: Jennifer Madison Davis
Assistant Managing Editor: Cathy Lu
Special Publications Manager: Risa Laib
Editors: Glenn Eriksen, Julie Fanselow, Tom Griffin, Suzanne Kotz, Rosie Leutzinger, Jessica Shaw, Carrie Shepherd
Editorial & Production Assistant: Megan Simms
Editorial Interns: Amelia Benich, Maxwell Eberle
Contributor: Gene Openshaw
Graphic Content Director: Sandra Hundacker
Maps & Graphics: David C. Hoerlein, Lauren Mills, Mary Rostad
Digital Asset Coordinator: Orin Dubrow

Avalon Travel

Senior Editor and Series Manager: Madhu Prasher
Editors: Jamie Andrade, Sierra Machado
Copy Editor: Maggie Ryan
Proofreader: Kelly Lydick, Patrick Collins
Indexer: Stephen Callahan
Production & Typesetting: Christine DeLorenzo, Lisi Baldwin, Rue Flaherty
Cover Design: Kimberly Glyder Design
Maps & Graphics: Kat Bennett

Let's Keep on Travelin'

Your trip doesn't need to end.

Follow Rick on social media!